THE MAGIC VOLCANO

MOLLY'S MAGICAL ADVENTURES: BOOK ONE

V.K. MAY

Copyright © 2021 by V.K. May

All rights reserved. No part of this book may be reproduced in any form or by any electronic or mechanical means, including information storage and retrieval systems, without written permission from the author, except for the use of brief quotations in a book review. Contact the author via: vkmay.com

This book has been published by Opal Tree Press.
ISBN: 978-1-9196363-0-6

Books in this series include -
The Magic Volcano: Book One
Jungle Magic: Book Two
Adaline's Magic: Book Three

WHO IS MOLLY MARSH?

Molly Marsh was born and raised in Calga, New South Wales, about 75 kilometers north of Sydney, Australia. She has never lived in the center of the town, but out a bit, in a quiet place surrounded by hills and bushlands. What she loves most about living there is the local wildlife park which she has been visiting almost every weekend, for as long as she can recall.

She is fascinated by plants and animals and believes she can speak with them. Her parents do not believe that is possible, but they are always amazed by the way animals respond to Molly.

'It's as though they recognize and trust her,' her mother once said to a friend while drinking coffee on their balcony which overlooked their rainforest garden.

Molly is a straight-A student, with science being her favorite subject. She is kind and sensitive to the feelings of other people, except when her curiosity takes over. In those situations, she can be quite annoying, but she does get to the bottom of things.

Her parents are professional people who love to travel during vacation time. Molly has always enjoyed their overseas holidays, even the time spent on planes. She loves flying, especially the moment when the plane lifts off the tarmac.

A NOTE TO READERS

Molly Marsh uses American spelling.

She also uses the metric system which works like this -
  1 meter = 1.1 yards OR 3.3 feet
  1 kilometer = 1,094 yard OR 3,2801 feet
  1 centimeter = 0.4 inch

1

MOLLY ON A PLANE

Molly Marsh loved to travel. But this journey was different from all the others. This time, she had said goodbye to her friends for a whole year. Then she had cried herself to sleep, clinging to her beloved cat, Kiki, who she would miss most of all.

The plane was headed for Papua New Guinea, the most unexplored country on Earth. Her father sat to her right, beside the window. His fingers fluttered over his laptop keyboard, reminding Molly of a flutter of butterflies. She imagined a dark shape outside the window. The body of a butterfly, perhaps. Another butterfly would appear, and then a third and maybe a fourth.

Soon, they would all be fluttering outside the window. This would be their way of saying 'hello', but the vibrations caused by their fluttering wings would crack the glass. It would start with one small crack and progress to an entire network of cracks that would branch out like the roots of a great tree. Then the window would turn to water and slosh all over her father's keyboard.

'Argh!' he would cry.

Then he would wipe his hands on his jeans, push his glasses up his shiny nose and continue typing. Even when the plane dipped and everyone screamed.

'Dad, the plane must have banged into a cloud,' said Molly, clutching her stomach.

Her father shoved his laptop under his seat and took hold of her hand.

'Are you okay, muppet?' he asked.

'I'm fine, thanks, Dad,' she replied. 'I know the plane won't crash.'

Her father smiled and winked at her.

'No, it won't,' he said.

Molly looked at her father's spiky red hair and the freckles on his nose, imagining him as a little boy. Which was strange, considering he was a very grown-up and serious father.

'Dad, are you looking forward to living in Papua New Guinea?' she asked.

Her father nodded.

'Yes, but I'll have a lot of work to do when we get there,' he replied.

'Do you like being a mining engineer?' Molly asked.

'Yep,' he said, nodding again.

Molly imagined her father staring at strange drawings of mines. She had seen him do it many times before, in their home in Australia. He would spread the big pieces of white paper across his workbench on the balcony and stare at them for ages. Sometimes Molly would look over his shoulder and see the silly squiggles, then wonder why he did not stare at their lovely garden instead.

'Will the drawings be the same as before?' she asked.

'Do you mean the mine schematics?' her father asked.

Molly nodded.

'Not really,' he replied. 'Every mine is different.'

'How?' Molly asked.

'Mostly, it depends on the type of mine - underground or open cut,' he replied. 'The ones you've seen in Australia were open cut.'

'Which type are we going to?' Molly asked.

'Underground,' her father replied.

'But *you* won't have to go under the ground, will you, Dad?' Molly asked.

'Sometimes,' he replied.

Molly saw her father's serious blue eyes brighten as the sun burst through a thin cloud. She tried to imagine him under the ground, then worried he might get lost, or that the ground might decide to keep him.

'I don't want you to go under the ground, Dad,' she said.

Her father kissed her hand.

'I'll be fine, muppet,' he said.

Molly hoped she could keep an eye on her father, but the thought of going under the ground did not make her feel good. She much preferred the fresh air and sunshine.

Her father smiled at her.

'Have you read the National Geographic articles we downloaded to your tablet?' he asked.

'Not yet,' Molly replied, reaching for her device.

She tapped the screen, then selected the black square with the yellow border. An article about PNG opened, and she started reading. She soon learned that most of the people in PNG live in small tribes, isolated from each other because of the vast mountains and thick jungle between them. This is why PNG is one of the least explored countries in the world, it said. Molly knew that was true because her mother had said the same thing, and she was a professor of anthropology at the University of Sydney. But she was asleep now, and unavailable for chatting, so Molly turned to her father again.

'Dad, did you know they have over eight hundred languages in PNG?' she asked.

'Hm?' her father replied, his eyes and hands finally reunited with his laptop. 'No problem, muppet. We only have to speak English.'

Molly swiped the screen of her device. A video appeared, showing five round huts made from mud, sticks, and leaves. They were arranged in a circle, which made her think the people who lived inside them must have been the best of friends. At the center of the circle was a pile of black ash and upon it were some logs, burning red. Perched upon the logs was a big round pot, with steam wafting out of it. Some tall, thin people wandered around. Their skin, almost as dark as the ash, was glistening with sweat. A pig, two dogs and five chickens lazed on the grass under the shade of a tree, showing no interest in anything the people were doing.

Next, Molly scrolled down to a photograph. It was a close-up of a man's face. She imagined him staring into her eyes, counting the blue and green flecks in her irises. But no matter how hard she stared at him, she could only see one color in his eyes, and it was dark brown. The long scars across his cheeks were wide and raised. Molly remembered her mother had told her that the mountain men of PNG had a tradition of deliberately cutting their faces. 'The scars are for decoration', her mother had explained, 'and badges of honor'.

Molly sat up, as high as she could, and gazed out of the window. She could see the mountains. They were covered in the soft green fur of the jungle and framed by the golden light of the rising sun. She stretched, but could not see much more.

'Come here, muppet,' her father said, lifting her out of her seat.

With her face pressed against the window, Molly could see some mountains that looked different from the others. They had no green fur, but were completely bare, revealing the red-brown rock from which they were made.

'It's a volcano!' she said.

'That's right,' her father replied. 'It's not active, though.'

'I wonder what's living down there,' said Molly.

'Maybe a few trees,' her father replied.

'You just never know, Dad,' Molly said, leaning into him. 'There could be more.'

Her father smiled.

'Molly Marsh, you really are the most imaginative person I have ever met,' he said.

Imaginative.

Molly pictured the word wriggling up and down like a caterpillar.

'Attention, passengers!' said the speaker above her head. 'We are commencing our descent. Please remain seated, fasten your seatbelts and ensure your tray tables are secured to the seat in front of you.'

2

YOU WILL LIKE IT HERE

As soon as Molly stepped off the plane, the hot air enveloped her like a steamy wet blanket. Her sandals filled with pools of sweat, making it difficult for her to walk across the tarmac. Her frizzy hair fell flat against her head and she had to squint under the bright sunlight.

Inside the airport, it was completely different. The air was close to freezing. Molly wondered if it was like that to help everyone cope with the fact that it was very crowded. There were so many people, and they were all walking in different directions, like a flock of seabirds that had just landed on a cliff.

One waddled over to Molly's father.

'G'day, Mr. Marsh,' he said, offering his hand.

'Jimbo!' said Molly's father, shaking the man's hand. 'This is my wife and daughter.'

'Ladies,' said Jimbo, nodding at Molly and her mother.

Too tired to respond, Molly just clung to her mother's hand, hoping they would soon escape the crowd. When the front door of the airport building slid open, she was once again enveloped by hot, damp air. For a moment it felt nice, like a hot water bottle on a chilly night. But the heat soon pressed down upon her, making her wish she could turn to water and trickle down a drain all the way to the sea.

When Molly stepped into the open carpark under the sun, a bright blue butterfly, just like those she had seen through the window of the plane, landed on her nose. It opened its wings, completely covering her face, and its long black antennae tapped her forehead.

'You will like it here,' it whispered.

Then it flew away.

Molly had always liked it when things like this happened. But this time she was not so sure because the butterfly was wrong. She was not going to like it here. Of that, she was certain.

On the outer edge of the car park, she saw a white van parked between two tall trees. It had a front seat and a back seat, like any family car. But there was also a long, open section at the back. She wondered if it might be for carrying long things, like trees or people who are too lazy to sit up straight.

'This is your van,' said Jimbo.

Leaning against the van was a tall, thin man who looked exactly like the man Molly had seen in the National Geographic article. Even from a distance, she could see the scars on his cheeks. He was wearing a white shirt with pale yellow flowers on it, and a pair of faded red shorts. He was not wearing any shoes, which made Molly wonder why the soles of his feet did not get burned by the hot ground. Between his fingers, he twirled a blade of grass.

'Hey!' Jimbo shouted.

The tall man threw the grass away and reached toward the suitcases.

'This is Yosia,' said Jimbo, pointing at the man. 'He comes with the van and the house.'

Molly's father offered his hand.

'G'day, mate,' he said.

The tall man put down the suitcases and shook Molly's father's hand.

'Good to meet you, Mr. Marsh,' he said.

Molly's mother stepped forward to offer her hand, but Yosia had already picked up the suitcases again. He piled them into the back of the van, then sat between them. Molly was about to ask him what he was doing, but her mother nudged her into the back seat. Molly fastened her seatbelt, then looked at Yosia, then at her mother.

'He doesn't have a seatbelt, Mum!' she whispered.

Her father glanced at Yosia, then at Jimbo.

'There's room in here for Yosia,' he said. 'Can we ask him to join us?'

Molly saw Jimbo's face turn red and press his lips together, forming a thin white line.

'Sorry, Mr. Marsh,' he replied. 'There are only four seatbelts in this vehicle.'

He started the van, and black smoke coughed out from the under the bonnet.

'Um,' said Molly's father, pointing to the thick cloud.

'No worries, Mr. Marsh,' Jimbo replied. 'It sometimes does that. You'll get used to it.'

3

EVERYTHING LOOKS DIFFERENT

As soon as they entered the highway, Molly could see the PNG sky was almost as bright as the Australian sky. But unlike the highways in Australia, this one was jumping with life. There were people wandering along the side of the road. Pigs and dogs trailed along behind them and chickens darted in between them. The road was crammed with cars, buses and trucks, all blowing black smoke out of their rears and honking their horns.

The van lifted off the road for a moment, then returned with a *thud!* Which made Molly and her mother scream. It felt even worse than the turbulence on the plane.

Jimbo turned his head ever so slightly.

'Sorry, ladies!' he shouted. 'The roads are full of potholes and bumps. You'll get used to it.'

Molly did not care what Jimbo had to say, because she had decided she did not like him. And she was still worried about Yosia. But when she looked again, she saw him lounging between the bags, looking as comfortable as someone in their favorite armchair watching TV.

Jimbo veered off the highway, taking them onto a narrow road and surrounded by open fields with only a few trees dotted around the landscape. Molly could see even more sky than before. In the distance, she saw a vast mountain range covered in thick jungle, and at the base of the mountains she saw a cluster of houses nestled between some palm trees.

She pointed at the houses.

'They look like boxes on legs,' she said.

'They're called *stilts*,' her mother replied. 'They keep the houses dry when floods come.'

As they got closer, Molly could see the stilts were much higher than her, which probably meant the floods would be higher than her, too. And that would mean she would have to swim around her neighborhood, which would get tiring after a while. She also worried that some people might not know how to swim so they would have to stay inside until everything dried out again.

'When's the flood coming?' she asked.

'It's not,' her mother replied. 'The stilts are just a precaution.'

Molly noticed every house had a luscious garden filled with trees of all shapes and sizes. And every tree was bursting with bright pink, red, orange and yellow flowers. There were lots of children on the road - riding bicycles, playing football and chatting - and Molly hoped they would become friends.

'This is it,' said Jimbo.

He turned the van off the road so sharply that Molly's head bumped into the window. Then he zoomed up the driveway so fast that Molly's mother gripped her stomach.

And for his grand finale, he slammed his foot on the brake so suddenly that everyone fell forward.

'Geez, Jimbo,' said Molly's father. 'That was quite a ride.'

Jimbo laughed so much that his shoulders and belly moved up and down.

4

MOLLY'S NEW HOME

Molly wanted to be the first one into the new house, but the adults and their longer legs were much faster. By the time she had climbed up the back steps and entered the back door, her parents and Jimbo were already standing around the dining table. Then Yosia entered, carrying more suitcases and a carton of food. Everyone stopped talking and stared at him, but he stared right back and then bowed to Molly's mother.

She stepped forward and shook his hand.

'Pleased to meet you, Yosia,' she said. 'I'm Mrs. Marsh and this my daughter, Molly.'

'Hi, Yosia,' said Molly, smiling.

Yosia looked at Molly then smiled so widely, the scars on his cheeks bent upwards, like two extra smiles. And his teeth were the brightest white that Molly had ever seen. Except for the red lines extending from his gums.

'Why do you have red stripes on your white teeth?' she asked.

Yosia laughed.

'I eat red berries,' he replied.

Jimbo glared at Yosia.

'No trouble from you, all right?' he said.

Yosia looked surprised, then confused, then embarrassed. Molly felt angry with Jimbo for being so rude and she was not surprised to see her parents frowning at him, too. His fat, red face and his bent nose reminded Molly of a pig. Not a cute pink pig, but a big ugly grey one with muddy feet and a squealing snout.

'You're very rude!' she shouted. 'Get out of our house!'

'Molly!' her parents both said, their faces falling.

Jimbo let out a cruel laugh that sounded like a crackling fire. Then he looked at Yosia.

'You heard the kid,' he said. 'Get out!'

'I was talking to *you!*' Molly shouted, jutting her chin toward Jimbo.

Molly's parents gasped. Molly knew this meant they were shocked and embarrassed by what she had just said to Jimbo. And that confused her because she knew her parents were just as angry with Jimbo and she was.

'My apologies, Jimbo,' her father said. 'Our daughter has a few impulse control issues.'

Jimbo tried to laugh but ended up doing a half-smile, half-grimace that just looked stupid.

'This might be a good time for you to take me to the mine,' said Molly's father.

'Righto,' said Jimbo, following him to the back door.

Molly was pleased to see Jimbo leave her house.

'I hope he pops like a balloon!' she said.

Yosia lifted Molly's suitcase, which looked more like a lunchbox in his huge hands.

'Follow me,' he said.

Molly and her mother followed him to a room at the end of the hallway.

'My new bedroom!' said Molly.

Yosia leaned Molly's suitcase against her bed, nodded, then left. Molly shifted it, then got a nasty fright. Something large and brown ran out from under her bed, then scuttled across the brown carpet. It moved so fast, she did not have time to understand what it was. But as it ran down the hallway, she knew exactly what she was looking at.

'Mum! There's a really big spider running down the hall!' she shouted.

She watched the critter turning into the lounge room, so she ran in the opposite direction - the kitchen - straight into her mother's arms.

'What's wrong?' her mother asked.

'I just saw a really big hairy spider!' Molly shouted.

Her mother shivered. Then her eyes turned dark, fixed on the kitchen floor. Molly saw the spider scrambling into the kitchen, straight toward her. It was then she realized it was as big as her foot.

'Yosia!' she screamed. 'Help!'

Yosia ran toward the kitchen where Molly stood, clinging to her mother's sweat-soaked shirt. Her mother lifted her hand slowly and pointed at the spider.

'Get rid of it!' she shouted.

Yosia leapt toward the critter but missed. The critter ran one way and then another, making Molly feel sick and sweaty. But when Yosia finally caught it, she felt relief wash over her like a cool shower.

'Thank you, Yosia,' her mother said. 'Now please, get rid

of it!'

Yosia clasped both of his hands around the spider. But even through his huge fingers, Molly could see the creature scrambling around in circles, desperate to break free.

'Throw it outside!' her mother screamed.

Yosia took two giant steps toward the back door, kicked it open, and gently placed the spider on the back step. But even from the kitchen, Molly could see it was not moving away. It lingered, as though waiting for a second chance to terrify everyone.

Yosia stood there, watching it.

'Okay, it's under the house now,' he said.

Molly made a note to herself to never go under the house. Not for anything.

'Yosia, please come in and close the door,' her mother called out.

Yosia stepped inside, giving the fly screen door a gentle tug. Molly watched it swing back behind him. What she saw next turned her blood to ice and made her tremble from head to toe. Clinging to the fly screen was a lizard occupying the entire width and length of the screen. Its head looked like a football with eyes and its long, pink tongue, forked like a snake's, flicked in and out of its mouth as though wondering what Molly and her mother would taste like.

Unable to speak, Molly just stood there, tugging her mother's shirt.

'What now?' her mother gasped.

Still trembling, she looked at the door and saw the massive lizard. Her eyes turned dark again, her mouth quivered, and then her entire body trembled.

'What. Is. That?' she said, her voice dripping with terror.

Yosia turned to look at the back door.

'Oh, that's Ted,' he said. 'He's harmless.'

He stepped over to the fly screen door and tapped the belly of the beast, just as casually as Molly would have brushed an ant off the table. Slowly, the lizard unlatched his claws from the door and ambled away. His long, thick tail dragged behind him as he clattered up the external wall of the house, then onto the roof.

Molly shot a look at Yosia.

'Do you know that beast?' she asked.

Yosia nodded and smiled.

'Yes, Ted's lived here for decades,' he replied.

Molly and her mother stared into each other's wide and terrified eyes. Yosia took one look at them, then rushed into the kitchen. He grabbed two glasses from the cupboard and filled them with water.

'Please drink,' he said.

Slowly, Molly sipped the water, trying to relax enough to swallow. Then she stared at Yosia, grateful he was there. His warm, round eyes stared back at her as he took the glass from her trembling hands. Molly looked at her mother, noticing her skin had turned a pale shade of grey.

'It's okay, Mum,' she said.

Her mother placed her glass on the kitchen bench, her hand still trembling. Molly took in a deep breath, then let it out, loud and slow. Her mother did the same, then wiped the sweat off her face. They looked at each other and exchanged weak smiles, but neither spoke.

'I'll be back to help you with dinner,' said Yosia.

5

YOSIA'S HOME

Molly wandered down the center of her long garden, between the thick rows of flowering trees on either side. She noticed how lovely they were, but her eyes were fixed on the brown, cone-shaped hut down at the end of the garden. Nestled among several large trees, it was a private place, she could tell. But she was curious, so she kept walking toward it.

When she arrived, she wanted to knock on the door. But there was no door, only a thick black sheet nailed to the external wall. She did not know what to do, so she was pleased when Yosia stepped outside.

He sat on a giant pumpkin next to the entrance and rested his elbows on his knees.

'Hi, Molly,' he said.

'Is this your home?' Molly asked.

'Yes,' he replied.

'Can I see inside?' she asked.

'No.'

'Can I sit here and chat with you?' she asked.

'Of course,' Yosia replied.

Molly sat on the thick grass and looked up at the trees snuggled around Yosia's hut. There were so many branches, she quickly lost track of which ones came from which tree. Between the leaves she saw a brown bird staring at her. It was a plain brown female, and Molly got the feeling there was something special about her.

'That's a beautiful bird,' she said, pointing.

Yosia nodded.

'Your hut is nice, too,' Molly added.

Yosia nodded again.

'Do you have an oven in there?' Molly asked.

'No,' Yosia replied.

'What do you eat?' she asked.

'Fruits, berries and vegetables,' he replied. 'Sometimes bread and beer.'

'How do you cook the bread?' Molly asked.

'There,' said Yosia, pointing to a pile of ash on the ground.

He picked up a round, flat wooden bowl and placed it on his lap. Then he lifted the wooden spoon resting inside it and used it to beat, squash and smooth some red berries into a paste.

'See?' he said, tilting the bowl so Molly could see inside.

He stepped inside his hut, then returned a moment later with a loaf of bread. He tore away a piece, smeared the red paste across it, then handed it to Molly. She took a bite, surprised by how great it tasted.

'Good?' he asked.

'Mm,' said Molly, chewing hard.

Yosia tore off another piece of bread, spread some paste

across it and threw it into his mouth. Molly watched his huge jaw crunching down like a crocodile that had just caught its last meal. And when he swallowed, all the veins bulged from the side of his skinny neck.

'More?' he asked, lifting the bowl onto his lap again.

Molly shook her head.

'Mum will be cross with me if I don't eat my dinner,' she said.

Yosia nodded, then kept eating.

Molly listened to the orchestra of birds chirping in the trees.

'Excuse me,' she said, standing up.

She walked toward the row of hibiscus trees that separated her garden from the neighbours' garden. Covered in hot pink flowers, they were a beautiful sight. She reached toward one, but a butterfly got in the way. It landed on the outer edge of the petal and stuck its long black antennae into the center of the flower while its tiny black feet gripped the petal. Molly wanted to touch its luminous blue wings, certain they would feel like silk, but she sensed the butterfly would not like that. So she put her hands behind her back and watched, almost afraid to breathe in case she scared the creature away.

A moment later, it retreated from the center of the flower and looked at her.

'Do you like it here?' it asked.

'Yes,' Molly replied, reaching toward it.

But before she could blink, the butterfly was gone.

6

THE BUTTERFLIES NEED HELP

Through the trees, Molly heard an unfamiliar voice.

'Gotcha!' it said.

She peered between the branches and saw a boy. He was on his knees, holding a white net. Through the net, Molly could see a brilliant blue butterfly. Its wings were beating fast, like an electric drum that was too fast to dance to.

'Help!' it screamed.

Molly ran toward the boy.

'What are you doing?' she shouted.

The boy looked up, his mouth gaping open.

'What's it look like I'm doing?' he said, placing the butterfly inside an empty glass jar.

'Stop it!' Molly shouted.

The boy glanced at Molly again, frowned, then took a step back.

'You can't do that!' Molly shouted. 'Let it go!'

The boy turned away, then ran toward his house, clutching his jar.

'Come back here!' Molly shouted.

She followed him all the way up the back steps.

'You can't do that!' she shouted.

When the boy reached his back door, he glared at Molly as though she was the most disgusting thing on the planet.

'Get away!' he shrieked.

He rushed inside and tried to close the door in Molly's face, but she pushed her way in. The radio was screeching in the kitchen and the TV was booming from the lounge room, creating a confusing mix of sounds that made Molly want to run away. But she could not leave, because the butterfly had begged her for help.

'Get out!' the boy shrieked. 'This is not your house!'

'And this is not your butterfly!' Molly replied.

The boy's chin quivered, like he was about to cry.

'I'm not trying to frighten you,' said Molly.

The boy scoffed.

'I'm not frightened of you!' he shrieked.

'Good,' said Molly. 'Now, let the butterfly go.'

'No!' he shouted.

He stomped down the hallway, then kicked his bedroom door open. Molly followed, and what she saw next made her feel sick and sad. From the floor to the ceiling, the wall was covered in corkboard and upon it were hundreds of dead butterflies, pinned in neat rows. Her eyes burned with tears as she tried to understand how anyone could do such a horrible thing.

'It's not a big deal,' said the boy, pointing to another glass jar on his desk.

'It's murder!' Molly screamed.

The boy scoffed, then shook his head.

'It's really simple,' he said. 'Inside this jar is a cloth that's been soaked with white spirits. When I drop the cloth into the jar with the butterflies, they breathe in the fumes and go to sleep.'

'They don't go to sleep, you idiot!' Molly shouted. 'They die!'

The boy shrugged his shoulders.

'Same thing,' he said.

He picked up the jar containing the butterfly he had just caught. Its wings were still beating fast, and Molly could hear it crying out for help.

'Please let it go,' she cried.

But the boy unscrewed the lid and dropped the tiny piece of cloth inside.

'No!' Molly shouted, pulling at his arm.

The boy screwed the lid on tight.

'Please help me!' the butterfly called out.

Molly reached for the jar, but the boy pulled it from her hands, and she fell to the floor. Through her tears, she could see the butterfly's wings beating slower.

'Please, stop!' she cried again.

But it was too late. The butterfly's wings had stopped moving. Then it fell sideways, across the bottom of the jar.

'One, two, three, four, five,' said the boy.

He opened the jar, picked up the dead butterfly and pinned it to the corkboard.

'Ta-dah!' he said, standing in front of his sick collection.

'You're a very cruel boy,' said Molly. 'I wish I'd never met you.'

She ran to the door, but the boy grabbed her arm. She pulled away, but he hung on tighter.

'Let me go!' she shrieked.

'Hang on!' he shouted. 'I want to show you something else.'

'Let me go!' Molly shouted.

She finally pulled free of the boy's grip just as his bedroom door flung open. Yosia stepped in, his forehead creased with a deep frown and his eyes burning with rage. But Molly was not afraid of him. She knew he had come to help.

7

YOSIA'S MAGIC

Molly was not sure how much time had passed. She saw the boy sitting on the edge of his bed, unable to move. Only his eyes could move, and they were darting around the room just as wildly as the butterfly's wings had when it was trapped inside his jar.

Everything had gone quiet. The birds outside were no longer chirping, the children on the street were no longer laughing, and the TV and radio were no longer broadcasting. The air had become thick and dark. Until one of the butterflies moved its wings, causing a swirl of light to waft around the room. Another did the same thing. And then another.

Soon, all the butterflies were wriggling free from their cruel pins and filling the room with their vibrant blue flutter. Molly squealed with delight, then jumped up and down, clapping her hands. A warm and tingling sensation travelled through her body, making her feel happier than she had ever felt before. She opened the window and watched the first brave butterfly escape.

'I'm going to watch this from outside!' she said.

The boy's eyes, almost the size of saucers, stared at her. Molly knew he was asking for help, but she did not care. The boy had not cared when the butterfly had begged him to stop killing it, so she felt no need to help him now.

She bent down and brought her face closer to his.

'Now you know how it feels to be helpless,' she whispered.

Then she ran from the boy's house, with Yosia right behind her.

Before Molly knew it, she was standing in her garden, staring up at the boy's bedroom window. She saw hundreds of the lovely blue creatures fluttering outside, gathering at the top of his house. Their wings sounded like a band of wild drummers, and they cast an electric blue glow across the roof that made her squint. Next, they assembled in a spiral formation and flew high into the sky. Where they were going, she did not know. She dared to hope they had gone to another realm, a more magical one reserved for only the brightest and bravest of butterflies.

Molly looked around, relieved the boy was nowhere to be seen. Then she looked at Yosia, sitting on his pumpkin outside his hut. He smiled and waved then continued to beat, squash and smooth some berries into a tasty paste.

8

THE MARSH FAMILY DINNER

The Marsh family decided to have an early dinner. Yosia set the table exactly the way Molly's mother liked it. When he finished, he opened the back door and stepped out.

'Yosia, will you join us?' asked Molly's mother.

For a moment, Yosia just stood there, with one foot out of the door and the other still inside the house. He did not say or do anything. But when he glanced at Molly, and she smiled and nodded, he did the same.

'Thank you, Mrs. Marsh,' he replied, closing the back door. 'I'd love to.'

'Why else would we have asked you to set four places?' said Molly, smiling at him.

Yosia seemed awkward as he sat down, but Molly was glad he was joining her family for dinner because she had decided she liked him very much.

'Can I get you a drink, mate?' her father asked.

Yosia seemed too surprised to answer the question, but he smiled wide when Molly's father placed a tall glass of juice in front of him.

'Dig in, everyone,' said Molly's mother, placing a huge metal tray in the center of the table.

Upon it was a crispy golden chicken with steam rising from every millimeter of its skin, filling the room with the scent of lemon, thyme, butter and garlic. Around the bird was a ring of roast potatoes, pumpkin, sweet potato, parsnips and beetroot, all of Molly's favorites. Next, her mother placed a large jug of gravy on the table, and that was Molly's cue to start filling her plate.

'How was everyone's day?' her mother asked, sitting down.

Molly and Yosia exchanged glances, then looked at Molly's mother.

'Well, today we met a massive lizard called Ted,' said Molly.

Her father frowned for a moment, then seemed to understand.

'I've heard about that thing,' he said. 'Apparently it's lived here for years!'

Yosia nodded, but Molly's mother glared at her husband.

'You could have warned me, darling,' she said.

Then she stabbed a potato with her fork.

Molly decided it might be a good idea to talk about something else.

'This morning, Yosia made some dead butterflies come back to life,' she said.

Her parents smiled, then winked at Yosia, but Molly knew that was just something they did when they did not believe what she was saying. They had never believed in magic, and that had always bothered her. But she knew what she had seen, and she was not afraid to talk about it. She glanced at Yosia, hoping he would agree with her, but he was busy chasing a slice of roast parsnip around his plate. Next, Molly's mind drifted back to earlier in the day, when they had first arrived at the house. Jimbo had left the house with her father and taken him to the mine.

'How was your first day in the mine, Dad?' Molly asked.

'Not good,' her father replied. 'Jimbo picked a fight with some lads and things got nasty.'

Yosia, Molly and her mother all glanced at other, each knowing what the other was thinking - *that's not difficult to imagine.*

'Well, I hope he got what he deserved,' said Molly, stabbing the chicken's chest.

Her father frowned at her.

'Ease up, Molly,' he said. 'There's no need to get stroppy.'

'Jimbo was rude to Yosia,' Molly argued.

'Yes, he was,' her father agreed.

Then he looked at Yosia.

'I really must apologise to you for that, Yosia,' he said.

Yosia's eyes watered for a moment, then he nodded.

'Jimbo can be a very unpleasant fellow,' Molly's father continued.

'Why does the company tolerate him?' her mother asked, scowling.

'He's a hard worker, and he gets the job done,' her father replied.

'What's his job?' Molly asked.

'Supervisor of the Rock Crushing Team,' her father replied.

Molly scoffed. She could easily imagine Jimbo crushing

rocks because he seemed to enjoy crushing people, too. More than anything, she wanted to live in a world filled with people who are kind. And Jimbo, she knew, was not one of those people. Neither was the boy next door, for that matter.

9

THE BOY WITH THE MOON FACE

A *ting!* sound rang through Molly's bedroom. She woke for just a moment, then returned to sleep. But the second *ting!* made her open her eyes and look at her clock. It was almost 10 p.m.

The third *ting!* got her out of bed. She gazed out of her window, at a vast and deep indigo sky wrapped around a moon so small, she thought it looked like a toenail clipping. The air was still, and the only sound she heard was the *click-clack* of the insects in her garden. Until the fourth *ting!* came.

This time, Molly saw a pebble bounce off her window. Someone was outside, she knew, and they wanted her attention, so she opened her window and looked down to the ground. There she saw the boy from next door. The boy who hunted and killed butterflies. The boy who had refused to stop, no matter how many times she had asked him to. The boy who had been overpowered by Yosia's magic earlier that day.

'What do *you* want?' she snapped.

'Please, can I speak with you?' he whispered.

'No way!' Molly shouted.

'Please,' he said, staring up at her.

Molly thought the boy's pale, round face looked like a full moon, and just as lonely.

'Okay,' she groaned.

A few moments later, she was standing outside, looking at the boy. His eyes and nose were red, and his mouth was quivering.

'Are you okay?' Molly asked.

'No,' he replied, wiping his eyes. 'I need to talk about what happened this afternoon.'

Molly rolled her eyes.

'Okay,' she said, folding her arms.

The boy scratched his forehead.

'I'm still trying to understand it,' he said.

Molly thought he must have been referring to the moment Yosia freed the butterflies.

'Do you mean Yosia's magic?' she asked.

The boy frowned and his lips pressed together into a thin line.

'If that's what you call it,' he said.

'That's *exactly* what I call it,' said Molly. 'But Yosia would call it science.'

The boy's eyes widened as though his eyeballs were planning to pop out of his head.

'It's not normal!' he hissed. 'What happened was not normal!'

'It was magic,' Molly insisted. 'And magic is real.'

The boy rubbed his forehead again.

'No, it's not,' he said.

Molly turned away from him, preparing to leave.

'Wait!' he said. 'Please, just help me understand - how do dead things come back to life?'

Molly smiled as she remembered the moment the butterflies had sprung back to life. Watching them fly out of the boy's bedroom widow had made her heart sing, and she could not imagine why anyone would feel differently. But this boy was different. And strange.

'What's your name, anyway?' she asked.

'Michael,' the boy replied.

'Okay, Michael,' she said. 'Let's start with you explaining why you killed those butterflies.'

Michael shrugged, then looked down at the ground.

'I like them,' he replied.

Molly scoffed.

'You can like them a lot more when they're flying free,' she said.

Michael did not respond, so Molly took a step closer, jutting her chin toward him. It was then she realized the top of her head was only as high as his shoulder, but she was not afraid of him.

'I told you not to kill them,' she said. 'I tried to stop you, but you did it anyway.'

Michael's eyes watered.

'I know,' he said. 'I feel bad about what I did.'

'Why did you do it?' Molly asked again.

'Just lonely, I guess,' he replied.

'Lonely?' Molly echoed. 'Don't you have any friends?'

'Not really,' Michael replied, shaking his head. 'The kids on this street just want to play football and video games and I'm not into those things.'

'Those things are boring,' said Molly.

'They are,' Michael agreed.

'What do you like doing?' Molly asked.

'Reading National Geographic articles and being outdoors,' Michael replied.

'Me too,' said Molly. 'I love discovering things in nature.'

Michael's face lit up, then he smiled.

'Do you think we could hang out sometime?' he asked.

Molly felt sorry for the boy because he seemed to be nice enough, and he was sorry for what he had done, but she did not want to hang out with anyone who had killed so many butterflies.

'Please,' he said.

Molly looked into Michael's sad and watery eyes.

'Please,' he said again.

'I'll make a deal with you,' said Molly.

'What?' said Michael, standing up straighter.

'I'll hang out with you if you promise to never harm another creature again,' she said.

Michael nodded.

'Do we have a deal?' she asked.

'Deal,' said Michael.

10

TWO FATHERS AND YOSIA

Molly decided to prove she had forgiven Michael by inviting him to join her for breakfast. He had been shy at first, but soon tucked into the pancakes with gusto. In fact, he had eaten so many that Molly's parents had glanced at each other with raised eyebrows.

Laying in Molly's garden now, he was rubbing his tummy and groaning.

'It serves you right for eating so much,' said Molly.

'I know,' Michael whined. 'But to be fair, your mum's pancakes are awesome!'

'True,' Molly giggled.

She lay down and closed her eyes. The thick grass under the picnic blanket made her feel like she was floating a few centimeters above the ground. Her face was in the shade. The tiny hairs on her arms were swaying in the breeze, and the rhythmic *click-clack* of the garden insects was making her smile. Until a screeching sound pierced the air.

Molly sat up and looked around.

'What's that?' she asked.

The noise cut through the air again, but this time, Molly knew where it had come from. Michael. He was snoring. She could hardly believe he had fallen asleep so quickly. Yosia walked past, so she called out to him. He smiled and nodded, but kept walking to the top of the garden. There he met Molly's father and another man. Molly guessed the man was Michael's father, so she gave the boy a nudge.

'Hm? What?' he said.

Then he sat up and gazed at the three men. Molly stared at them, too. She noticed they all said: 'good morning' and 'how are you?' and shook hands. The two fathers were standing with their legs apart and their arms folded across their chests. Yosia's posture was more relaxed, with one hand on his hip and the other dangling loosely by his side.

'Adults are weird, aren't they?' Molly whispered.

'Heck yeah,' said Michael.

Yosia started speaking and waving his arms around.

'I haven't seen him do that before,' said Michael.

Molly laughed.

'Like I said before - adults are weird,' she said.

The two fathers nodded at Yosia, then slowly moved away.

'Okay, thanks, mate,' said Molly's father.

Then he approached.

'Hey, kids,' he said.

'Good morning, Dad,' Molly replied.

'G'day, mate,' said the other man, rubbing Michael's head.

The boy's woolly hair stood on end, which made Molly laugh. Michael grunted, then smoothed it down again, which made his father laugh.

'It's good to meet you, Molly,' said the big man, offering his hand.

Molly stood up and shook the man's hand.

'And you, Mr. Calthorpe,' she replied.

Michael struggled to his feet, too.

'What's up, Dad?' he asked.

'We thought you two might like to have a look inside the mine,' Mr. Calthorpe replied.

Molly had often wished her father would tell her more about his work, especially because it took up so much of his time. But the thought of going under the ground made her feel nervous.

Michael seemed to feel differently.

'That would be brilliant!' he said. 'When do we go?'

'Now,' said Mr. Calthorpe.

11

A STRUGGLE THROUGH THE JUNGLE

Molly soon found herself walking down her street with Michael by her side and their fathers a few steps ahead. Ted was behind her, his claws clattering along the bitumen road. She felt flattered that the beast had started following her everywhere, like a pet dog, but she found him weird and creepy.

Her eyes were on Mr. Calthorpe, about half a meter ahead. Like Michael, the man was big and round. But unlike Michael, he walked with a limp. Molly wondered if that was because his body was too large for his legs, like the houses on stilts. Then she gazed around the houses, noticing they were bigger and more freshly painted than hers and Michael's.

'Even the stilts have a thick coat of white paint,' she said, pointing at one house.

'Yeah, it's posh down here,' said Michael.

Molly's father glanced over his shoulder.

'The owners of the mine live down here,' he said. 'So please behave yourself.'

'There doesn't *seem* to be anyone living here,' Molly whispered.

'I know,' Michael whispered back. 'There are never any kids playing out the front, and I've never seen anyone driving in or out. Maybe it's just rich ghosts that live here.'

'They work incredibly long hours,' said Mr. Calthorpe.

'So that means we *can* misbehave,' Molly said, smiling at her father.

He glanced at her with a half-smile, half-frown that looked goofy. Molly was about to laugh at him when she realized they were walking straight toward a cluster of thick bushes at the end of the street.

'Where are we going?' she asked.

'Relax, muppet,' her father replied. 'There's no house behind these bushes. We just have to squeeze through them to get to the mine.'

'Isn't there a proper path?' Molly asked.

'Behind the bushes there is,' Michael replied.

'Have you been here before?' she asked.

'Once,' Michael replied. 'I helped Mum carry some equipment, then she sent me home.'

Molly watched Mr. Calthorpe struggle to squeeze between the trees. He could hardly bend and he got scratched by all the wild branches. Michael went next and he, too, struggled. After that, it was Molly's turn. She found it much easier, but she was glad her father was right behind her, just in case things got tricky. Which they did. Michael let one of the branches to flick back behind him and it slapped the tip of Molly's ear, sending a sharp stinging sensation around her entire scalp.

'Ow!' she screamed.

A STRUGGLE THROUGH THE JUNGLE   45

'Oh, muppet,' said her father, lifting her up.

He wrapped one arm around her back and the other underneath her, making her feel comfortable and safe. She rested her chin on his shoulder and gazed at Ted, ambling along the path behind her father. From the tip of his nose all the way to the tip of his tail, the lizard would have been at least three meters long, Molly guessed. And he was not very high, so he could scuttle between the bushes without any trouble.

'Oh, to be a lizard,' said Molly. 'Nothing is difficult.'

'I don't know about that,' her father said. 'Have you ever seen a lizard read a book? Or play the piano? Or dance in a ballet?'

Just picturing those things made Molly laugh out loud.

'You're funny, Dad,' she said, wrapping her arms around his neck.

When they arrived in a clearing, Molly's father lowered her to the ground. She looked around, guessing the path would have been about six meters across. The trees on both sides were tightly packed and showing off so many shapes and colors, she could not stop staring. She saw some coconut palms, some trees with shiny green leaves and bright red flowers, and others with smaller green leaves and pink and yellow flowers. Ferns, of all shapes and sizes, seemed to fill every millimeter of spare space. Ted wriggled between them, disappearing from view.

'This is beautiful!' Molly said.

'There's lots to look at,' Michael agreed.

'But not right now,' said Mr. Calthorpe. 'We're going this way.'

Molly watched the big man step into another thick

cluster of trees. Michael followed him and, a second later, they had both disappeared from view.

'Come on, muppet,' her father said.

He took Molly's hand and led her toward the trees. As she squeezed between them, Molly was relieved to find they were the soft and bendy type. The air was damp, too. She could feel the moisture on her skin and in her nose and mouth.

'This is better,' she said.

'Yes, it's an easier walk,' her father replied. 'The worst is behind us, muppet.'

The track was so narrow, Molly could see nothing but the back of her father's feet and the imprints that his shoes left on the ground. They were deep imprints which must have meant the ground was wet.

'Where's the water coming from?' she asked.

'Dunno,' her father replied. 'The only liquid around here is the pool of slurry and that's—'

'What's slurry?' Molly asked.

'It's a combination of water and sulfuric acid,' her father replied. 'We use it to extract the copper from the lumps of ore we pull from the mine.'

'Is that slurry stuff trickling through the jungle?' Molly asked.

'No, muppet, of course not,' her father replied. 'It's held in a big tight container.'

'The container must be leaking then, Dad, because the ground is damp,' Molly insisted.

'There's nothing wrong with the container, Molly,' he replied. 'It's checked regularly.'

Molly could feel that she and her father might be

heading for an argument, but she could not help herself. She had to understand the situation, and that meant asking questions.

'But what if the birds drink the slurry?' she asked. 'Won't it make them sick?'

'They *won't* drink it,' her father replied.

'How do you know?' Molly asked.

'They're not that stupid,' her father said.

'So, where is this container of slurry?' Molly asked.

'I can't tell you that, muppet,' he replied.

Molly could tell by the tone of her father's voice he was becoming fed up with her questions, so she decided to be quiet for a while. Her mind drifted back to something she had seen in science class in school. It was a series of photographs of an abandoned copper mine.

It had been an open cut mine, with circles carved deep into the surface of the earth. At its center, about two kilometers below the surface, had been a pool of bright blue-green water that had not looked natural. When she had asked about it, her science teacher had explained that sometimes the stuff gets into the drinking water and makes people sick.

Remembering all this made Molly feel angry.

'It's disgusting, Dad,' she said.

Her father glanced over his shoulder at her.

'What's disgusting?' he asked.

'Making all that dirty water and leaving it there,' Molly replied.

'There's nothing else we can do with it,' her father said. 'We can't send it out to the sea.'

'But we can stop mining, can't we?' Molly asked.

Her father scoffed.

'Do you enjoy having electricity?' he asked.

Molly could not imagine what electricity had to do with anything.

'Well, do you?' he asked again.

'Yes, but—' Molly started.

'Okay,' her father interrupted. 'Think of the electrical components in the circuit boards in your computer, tablet and TV, then tell me what you think they're made of.'

Molly had never given any thought to such things, but she was starting to get the idea.

'Are they made from copper?' she asked.

'That's right!' her father replied.

Molly knew her father was not one to tell tall tales. He was a man of facts and truth-telling. She admired him for that and had often tried to be more like him. But she was a girl who liked telling magical stories, so she was starting to realize she would never be like him.

She also knew there was no point in arguing, so she skipped over to him and shoved her little hand into his. He returned the love by giving her hand a gentle squeeze, which was just as well, because something moved under her shoes, and she slipped.

'The ground is definitely damp, Dad,' she said.

'Sorry, muppet,' said her father.

Molly clung to her father's hand with both of hers and kept her eyes on the ground. So when Mr. Calthorpe suddenly stopped, in the middle of the track, she almost walked into him. The man took up so much space, Molly could not see anything, so she looked up. She saw the top of a hill that would have been about as high as her house.

On top of the hill was a row of wide, flat, dark green leaves with only the thinnest slices of blue sky between them.

'Is that a banana orchard?' Molly asked, pointing at them.

'The collective noun for banana trees is *plantation*,' her father replied. 'And yes, it is.'

Molly imagined it would be difficult to climb those trees to collect the bananas. Just looking at them from the ground made her feel dizzy, so when Michael suddenly shouted, she almost fell over.

'Look at this!' he squealed.

Molly stepped around Mr. Calthorpe to see what Michael was so excited about. Standing at the boy's feet was a small, furry, chocolate brown colored creature. Its body was about the size of an adult male koala, but its face was more like a kangaroo's. Its tail was golden and furry.

'It's a tree kangaroo!' she said.

'That's right,' said Mr. Calthorpe. 'I'm not sure what it's doing this far inland.'

'It's hungry, Dad,' said Michael. 'We have to feed it.'

The lovely creature lifted its front paws off the ground and leaned back on its thick, golden tail, just as a kangaroo would do. Its pale blue eyes stared into Michael's and its fleshy pink nose twitched from side to side.

'Do we have any food, Dad?' Molly asked.

'Yes,' he replied, rummaging through his backpack.

Molly watched her father pull a brown paper bag out of his backpack.

'We have a mango and—' he started.

But before he could say any more, the tree kangaroo leapt up and snatched the mango from his hand. It scurried over to the nearest tree, its long tail bouncing up and down like a feather duster, then it raced up the tree trunk and disappeared among the leaves.

'Wow! That was fast,' Michael laughed.

'And beautiful,' said Molly, feeling her heart melt.

'Okay, guys, this is it!' said Mr. Calthorpe, pulling a set of keys from his pocket.

There were so many keys, and some were so big, Molly wondered how the man could walk with them all shoved into the pocket of his jeans. He fiddled with them for several seconds before he finally chose one, then he lumbered toward the dark hole in the side of the hill.

Michael followed.

'Is this really the entrance to the mine?' he asked.

'One of them,' Mr. Calthorpe replied.

The big man stooped to avoid banging his head on the rocks above the entrance, then he brought his key to the lock. It opened with a click then the gate opened with a groan.

12

THE LAKE INSIDE THE CAVE

Molly clung to her father as they stepped into the darkness.

'It's okay, muppet,' he said. 'Your eyes will adjust in a moment.'

Molly could hear him reaching for something beside her. She pressed her hand against the wall, noticing it was damp. There was no movement in the air which felt unnatural, so she was not looking forward to going deeper into the earth. Only her curiosity helped her take the next step.

'Hard hat,' her father said, placing one on her head.

'Thanks, Dad,' she replied.

'It's too big for you, but it will keep you safe,' he said, fastening the strap under her chin.

Molly moved her head from side to side, just to see what would happen. Sure enough, the oversized hat slid from side to side but did not fall off. Molly's eyes were adjusting to the darkness. She could see she was in a narrow tunnel and the only other people in sight were her father, Mr. Calthorpe and Michael.

'You'll need these too,' her father said, pulling a small pair of overalls from his backpack.

Molly stepped into the overalls, then inserted her arms and pulled the zipper up to her throat.

'They're comfy,' she said, suddenly feeling ready to handle whatever might come next.

'And these,' her father said, placing a pair of yellow rubber boots at her feet.

Molly slipped her feet into them, then pulled hard. So hard, she fell backward. If it had not been for her father standing behind her with his hands on her back, she would have landed on her butt.

'Well done, muppet,' he said. 'You've got them on.'

The tops of the boots pressed into Molly's calf muscles. She wriggled her toes around, noticing how strange they felt inside the boots, like hands inside a pair of boxing gloves.

'I didn't know you had all this gear, Dad,' she said.

'We ordered it especially for you guys,' he replied.

Molly glanced at Michael - a round shape with two shiny eyes - dressed the same as her. He was not doing anything, or saying anything, so Molly wondered if he was afraid of going under the ground. But now was not the time to ask questions like that, she knew.

'You look ready for action,' she said.

'Yep,' he replied with a nod.

'One last thing,' said Mr. Calthorpe.

He wrapped a mask around his nose and mouth, then wrapped another around Michael's face.

'What's it for, Mr. Calthorpe?' Molly asked.

'To keep out the dust and moderate the air quality,' he

replied. 'Here's one for you, and another one for your father.'

As Molly's father secured her mask to her face, she watched Mr. Calthorpe fix a small torch to his wrist. She expected him to give her one, too, but he did not. She waited a few more moments, but still, he did not give her a torch.

'Can I have a torch, too?' she asked.

The two fathers chuckled.

'Only the grown-ups get torches,' Mr. Calthorpe replied. 'They're expensive.'

Michael followed his father down the tunnel, and Molly followed Michael. Her father followed her, shining his torch on the ground at her feet. There was not much to see because the tunnel was narrow and completely dark, except for the small round circles of light from the torches.

'If the torches were better, they might give us bigger circles of light,' she said.

Molly heard her father chuckle behind her. Then Mr. Calthorpe moved his torch around so she could see the walls. They were glistening with water.

'Where's the water coming from?' she asked.

'You'll see,' said Mr. Calthorpe.

A moment later, they arrived at the end of the tunnel. Peering between Michael and his father, Molly saw a few slithers of light. She wanted to know where it was coming from, so she squeezed between the Calthorpe men and soon found herself staring into a cave.

'It must be the size of both of our houses put together!' she said.

'It's big, all right,' said Michael.

There were several lights shining on the ceiling and walls. They were a pale golden color with some bright blue stripes. Water trickled through the stripes, bringing the color to a bright blue lake below. The surface of the lake was so still, it reflected the ceiling, making the entire space look like something from a fairy tale.

'Is this real?' Molly whispered.

'Yep, this is a natural cave,' Mr. Calthorpe replied.

'What causes those blue stripes on the walls?' Michael asked.

'Copper sulfate,' Mr. Calthorpe replied. 'It's a natural byproduct of the copper in the rocks.'

'Do you use it for anything?' Michael asked.

'Pesticides,' Mr. Calthorpe replied. 'And medicines to treat bacterial and fungal infections.'

Then he winked at Molly.

'The sulfate also makes a beautiful crystal when it's cleaned up,' he said.

Molly gasped at the thought of having a crystal that color. She knew she would keep it on her bedside table so it would be the last thing she saw before she went to sleep every night and the first thing she saw every morning.

'They look like skinny blue ant hills!' said Michael.

Molly saw what Michael was pointing at. On the far side of the lake were several thin blue structures, probably about as high as her shoulders.

'There's so many of them!' she said.

'Do you guys know the proper name for those skinny ant hills?' her father asked.

Molly knew there was a word, but she could not remember it.

'Stalactites!' Michael shouted.

'Almost,' said Mr. Calthorpe. 'The word stalactite has the letter C in it, which can remind you of the word *ceiling*. But the ones on the ground—'

'Stalagmites!' Molly shouted.

'Well done!' said Mr. Calthorpe. 'The word stalagmite has the letter G in it which can remind you of the word *ground*. That's how you can remember the difference.'

Molly wanted to run her fingertips down the stalagmites, but they were too far away and there was a lake between them and her. She gazed at the lake again, marveling at how still it was. It reflected the ceiling of the cave so perfectly, the stalactites look like stalagmites, making the lake appear even more magical.

'How deep is that lake?' she asked.

'Good question,' her father replied. 'I have no idea.'

He looked at Mr. Calthorpe but the big man just shrugged his shoulders.

'Does anything live in there?' Molly asked.

'No,' her father replied. 'It contains far too much copper sulfate for anything to grow. And there's probably some sulfuric acid mixed in, too.'

'Sulfuric acid is what you use to extract the copper from the ore, right?' Molly asked.

'That's right, muppet,' her father replied.

'But you do the extraction work above the ground, don't you?' Michael asked.

Molly's father nodded then glanced at Mr. Calthorpe which made Molly wonder if there was something happening that should not be happening. Her father, she knew, was a very experience mining engineer, so he would know the answer to any question. Unless there was something strange going on.

And when she glanced at Mr. Calthorpe, she definitely got the feeling something was wrong because his mouth moved into an upside-down shape and he scratched his head.

'Yes, but the disturbance caused by mining activity can mix things up a bit,' he replied.

'Are you referring to the movements in the earth?' Molly asked.

Her father glanced at Mr. Calthorpe again.

'More or less, muppet,' he replied.

Molly wondered if her father was looking at Mr. Calthorpe, before answering her questions, because he was the husband of Mrs. Calthorpe, the big boss of the mine. And if so, maybe Mrs. Calthorpe knew something bad about the mine.

'Will the mining activity cause an earthquake, Dad?' she asked.

Her father glanced at Mr. Calthorpe again, then laughed gently.

'It's possible in theory, Molly,' said Mr. Calthorpe. 'But not likely.'

'There's one very important thing I must tell you, kids,' said Molly's father. 'Don't stick your hands in the lake! It won't do you any good at all. Understood?'

Molly and Michael nodded.

'In fact, it would be best if you refrained from touching anything,' said Mr. Calthorpe. 'Okay?'

'Okay,' Molly and Michael mumbled.

Molly could see a little wooden bridge across the lake,

and she was certain they would soon be walking over it because there was nowhere else to go. But she was not certain the bridge would take Mr. Calthorpe's weight, so she held her breath when the big man took his first step. And she almost stopped breathing when he took his second step because the bridge started to wobble. Then Michael followed his father.

It was Molly's turn, next, but she did not step forward because she wanted Mr. Calthorpe to arrive safely on the other side, first. She lingered for a moment, gazing at the lake. It was so perfectly still, she imagined what it would look like if the Loch Ness Monster broke through the surface. Its big black head would appear first, she imagined. Then, like a periscope on a submarine, it would swivel around and scan its surroundings. After that, it would slowly rise up, showing off its first hump. By then, everyone else would have noticed it and they would be taking photos with their phones. If their flashes did not go off, Nessie might even rise up a bit more.

Molly's interesting daydream was interrupted by her father nudging her.

'Come on, muppet,' he said.

Molly looked to the other end of the bridge. Michael and his father were there, waving at her, so she took her first step. When she got halfway across, she stopped and stared into the water, hoping to see a darker color, or something moving, but there was no change. It looked exactly the same as before - a milky, turquoise, chemical soup.

13

INTO THE BELLY OF THE MINE

Molly's thigh muscles ached from walking downhill. There was not much light ahead of her, but from what she could see, this tunnel was just as narrow as the last one. The air seemed to be warmer and wetter and even more unpleasant than before.

'What's that horrible smell?' she asked.

'Nothing in particular,' her father replied. 'It's just the lack of fresh air. Don't worry, muppet. We'll soon enter a place with big fans.'

'Fans?' Molly echoed. 'But there's no electricity down here.'

'Sure there is,' said Michael. 'You saw the lights shining around the cave, didn't you?'

Mr. Calthorpe joined the discussion.

'No, mate,' he said. 'Those lights were diesel powered. The same is true of the fans that Mr. Marsh just mentioned.'

Molly was glad to hear this because she did not like the idea of electrical cables in a mine that had so much water. Nor did she like the idea of an earthquake in a place that had electricity because that would cause an electrical fire. She remembered the day the Fire Brigade had visited her school and talked about the different types of fire. Electrical fires, they had said, always did the most damage.

'I'm glad there's no electricity down here, Dad,' she said. 'If there was, I would have to stop you from coming to work.'

Her father laughed, which she did not mind, because she knew she had been cheeky. But she was not happy about him working in this place. What if he got lost under the ground? What if there was an earthquake, and the ceiling fell on top of him? She imagined so many terrible things that she got a nasty shock when there was a tremor in the earth.

'What was that?' she shouted.

Then she heard some strange clanging and whirring noises.

'What was that?' she asked again.

'Sorry, muppet,' her father replied. 'I should have warned you about the machines. You'll see them when we reach the end of this tunnel.'

'What machines?' Michael asked.

'Haul trucks and cranes,' Mr. Calthorpe replied.

'Trucks and cranes?' Molly echoed. 'How did they get down here?'

'There's another entrance,' her father replied. 'Bigger than the one we just came through.'

Considering the narrow tunnel she was in, Molly could not imagine an entrance big enough for a truck to drive through. But she did not have to imagine for much longer, because she soon found herself staring into a massive open space that was filled with them.

'They're as big as the dinosaurs!' she shrieked.

'Bigger!' Michael shouted.

A huge yellow machine rolled forward on two long flat black belts that looked like giant skis. Its long neck must have been taller than ten giraffes, and it pointed straight up toward the ceiling. Another long yellow piece dangled down, and at the end of it was a large flat black tray. Molly pointed at it, then looked at Michael.

'That's an excavation crane,' he explained. 'Those guys over there are about to shovel rocks onto that tray. When it's full, the crane will dump the rocks into the back of that orange haul truck over there.'

Molly looked at the orange truck and could hardly believe her eyes. The thing was so high, there was even a stepladder up the front of it. And at the top of the steps was a platform, and on the platform was a cabin, and inside the cabin was a tiny person.

'Is that the truck driver?' she asked, pointing.

'Yeah!' said Michael.

'He looks like a piece of Lego,' Molly giggled.

But Michael did not think it was funny.

'The driver only looks small because the truck is so massive,' he said. 'It's so massive, Molly, if you were standing beside it, the top of your head would not even reach the top of its wheels.'

Molly watched the excavation crane lower its flat tray to the ground. Four men huddled around the tray and shoveled rocks onto it, making a sound like lots of earthquakes happening all at once. She recognized one of the men. It was Jimbo, the awful man who had collected her family at the airport and been rude to Yosia. She hoped he would not see her, so she hid behind her father. And when two more trucks drove into the space, making the ground shake, she pressed her hands over her ears and buried her face in the side of her father's belly.

'Are you okay?' he asked, rubbing her back.

Molly shook her head.

'Shall we get out of here?' her father asked.

Molly nodded. She'd had enough. She wanted to be on the couch with her mother, watching something silly on TV and eating popcorn. Or ice cream. Or both.

'Henry, we're going to head home,' her father shouted over the noise.

Mr. Calthorpe nodded at Molly's father. Then he then stepped toward Molly with a kind smile on his face. He opened his mouth so Molly knew he wanted to say something to her. She also knew he would shout to be heard over the noise, so she was not surprised when he stooped down toward her. But when he placed his entire body weight on one leg, all Molly heard was his scream. Then he fell to the ground, gripping his knee.

14

A HAUL TRUCK TO THE RESCUE

Molly's face was still buried in her father's waist when the medic arrived. She was a short woman wearing brown pants, a white shirt, and a dark blue cap. She had shiny brown skin, big brown eyes, and curly black hair.

She knelt beside Mr. Calthorpe, looking worried.

'Can you move?' she asked.

Mr. Calthorpe tried to get up but could not. His big round face was red and sweaty and pinched into a tight knot. Michael was on the ground beside him, resting his hands on his shoulder.

'Hang in there, Dad,' he said.

The medic unclipped a radio from her belt, then held it to her mouth.

'We need an emergency evac,' she shouted.

Molly heard someone respond through the radio, but she could not tell what they were saying. She only knew it was bad news because the medic frowned so deep, she could no longer see the woman's eyes.

'You're kidding,' said the medic.

She clipped the radio onto her belt and stared at the ground.

'What's wrong?' Molly's father asked.

The medic looked at him, her mouth down-turned.

'We only have one evac unit and it's on the road,' she replied.

Molly's father inhaled deep and loud.

'Plan B?' he asked, almost holding his breath.

The medic looked at the machines in the center of the space.

'Give me a moment,' she said.

Molly watched the medic approach the excavation crane, waving her hands at the driver. A moment later, the crane stopped moving, the cabin door opened, and a woman with spiky grey hair jumped out. She plonked a yellow hard hat on her head and strolled toward the medic. They spoke for a moment, then the medic returned.

This time, she looked even more worried.

'The only way we can get you to the surface is on that haul truck,' she said.

Molly could see that the back end of the truck was full of rocks and reversing, so it must have been preparing to drive to the surface.

'I can't climb up there!' said Mr. Calthorpe, clutching his knee.

'I know,' said the medic. 'But the crane can lift you.'

Mr. Calthorpe's face fell.

'Do it, Dad,' said Michael.

Mr. Calthorpe looked at Michael, then at the medic. Molly could tell he was wondering if there was some other way. She saw the man's eyes darting around the space, resting for a moment on each of the mechanical monsters, searching for an alternative solution. When his eyes stopped moving, Molly knew he had accepted his fate.

'Okay,' he grumbled.

The medic stood up, then looked at Molly and her father.

'Sorry, folks, but you must stand back,' she said. 'Over there, against the wall, please.'

Molly and her father retreated to the entrance of the tunnel from where they had come. This was a relief to Molly, because she was a few steps further away from the noise, the vibrations from the machines, and the shouting men.

The medic looked at Michael.

'Sorry, young man,' she said. 'I need you to step back, too.'

Michael looked up, his face stained with tears.

'He's my dad!' he cried. 'I'm not leaving him!'

The medic gave Michael's shoulder a squeeze.

'You can travel on the truck with your dad,' she said. 'But for now, I need you to stand back.'

Michael stood up slowly, then shuffled toward Molly, his eyes red. She put her arm around him and watched the four rock shoveling men approach Mr. Calthorpe. When they got closer, she knew for sure that one of them was Jimbo. He looked even more sweaty and messy than the last time she had seen him.

'Hey, Mr. Marsh,' he said, nodding at Molly's father.

'Jimbo, mate, how are you?' her father replied.

Jimbo just shrugged. Molly knew that probably meant

he thought he was not 'good' or 'bad' but something in between. But she thought he was bad. Very bad.

'Okay,' said the medic. 'I need one man under each shoulder and another man under each thigh. Do not bend his knees or try to straighten them, just hold them gently.'

'I don't think so,' said Jimbo, looking at Mr. Calthorpe who was almost twice his size.

'Just get on with it, mate,' said one of the other rock shoveling men.

Jimbo glared at the man, his fat lips curling into a sneer and his red face wobbling.

'And if I do my back in, will you pay for my time off work?' he snarled.

The other man clenched his fist, then released it a few times. Molly could feel the tension between the two men and she feared a fight might break out, so she shuffled closer to her father. Michael stepped forward with tears streaming down his face.

'Please help him!' he shouted.

Jimbo looked Michael up and down as though he were a lump of dirt he had just found on his bathroom floor. The other men nodded politely at Michael, but no one moved.

'I'll do it, then!' Michael shouted.

'No, you won't, young man,' said the medic, holding up her hand. 'These men are trained to lift, and that's what they're going to do!'

Then she glared at the four rock shoveling men.

'Please, gentlemen, just get on with it!' she said.

The four men bent down and placed their hands under Mr. Calthorpe's thighs and shoulders, then started to lift. Within seconds, their faces turned red and the veins on their necks bulged, but they got Mr. Calthorpe onto the tray. He lay back and let out a loud groan.

'Thanks, fellas,' he said.

Michael let out a tiny whimper of relief, and Molly squeezed his arm. She watched the crane lift the tray so high that Mr. Calthorpe's body was no longer visible. By the time the tray was level with the platform on the haul truck, the men were up there, and so was the medic. Slowly, they slid the big man onto the platform and he sprawled like a giant sack of potatoes. Then someone wrapped a rope around him.

'What are they doing?' Michael shrieked.

'It's okay,' said Molly's father. 'They're going to tie him to the railing so he doesn't slide off.'

The medic brought her radio to her mouth and spoke again. Every machine stopped and, for a few minutes, there was silence in the huge underground place. Molly sighed with relief. Then the medic waved Michael toward the truck.

The boy ran, like his life depended on it. Molly watched him getting smaller by the second. By the time he reached the bottom of the ladder of the huge orange haul truck, she thought he looked like an ant about to climb up the side of a jumbo box of tissues. She laughed, then wrapped her arms around her father's waist and watched the truck slowly exit the space through a big dark tunnel.

15

THE RING OF FIRE

Molly felt relieved to be back outside in the fresh air. She ran her fingers through her hair, unsticking it from her scalp. She was glad to be rid of the boots, too, because they had started to pinch her toes. But more than anything, she was relieved to be away from the noise and the bad-tempered men in the belly of the mine.

'I wish you didn't have to go down there, Dad,' she said.

'I'm sorry, muppet,' he replied. 'I wasn't expecting things to become so unpleasant today.'

'That's okay, Dad,' Molly replied. 'It was a good idea that you and Mr. Calthorpe had. I loved that cave and the bright blue lake. And Michael loved those big trucks.'

Her father smiled.

'That's good,' he said.

Molly clasped her hands around her father's forearm and skipped alongside him. She did not want to annoy him with too much conversation, but she was finding it difficult to be quiet.

'Do you *have* to work down there, Dad?' she asked.

Her father sighed.

'We've discussed this before, Molly,' he replied. 'I'm a mining engineer! This is what I do!'

'But it's dangerous, Dad,' she said. 'And the people are very unhappy.'

Her father did not reply, and she did not prompt him because she knew he was thinking about what she had just said. But she was glad when he finally spoke.

'Those people are unhappy,' he agreed. 'I'm not sure what's wrong down there.'

'Would Michael's mum know?' Molly asked. 'She's the big boss, isn't she?'

'Yep,' her father replied. 'I'll have a chat with her.'

Molly listened to the sound of her feet squelching across the damp jungle floor for a while. Until something else popped into her mind.

'Can I ask you a question, Dad?' she asked.

'Sure,' he replied.

'All the movement in the earth,' she started. 'I understand it's caused by the machines, and by pulling lumps of rock out of the ground, but don't you worry it might cause an earthquake?'

Her father stopped walking and stared at her.

'Molly, what is it with you and earthquakes?' he said.

'Sorry, Dad,' she sighed. 'It's just that there's a lot of research showing the link between mining and earthquakes.'

Her father frowned at her, so she decided to explain.

'Okay, so the mining activity shakes the ground and—'

'Excuse me, Little Miss,' her father said. 'I am a mining engineer. You do not have to explain the science to me as though I am a child. YOU are the child. I am the parent. If it wasn't safe for us to be here, I wouldn't have brought us here! Do. You. Understand?'

Molly felt bad. She did not like to upset people, least of all her parents.

'I understand, Dad,' she said. 'And I know you know what's best.'

But Molly knew she was right. And it was not fair that her father was getting so grouchy with her. She let go of his arm and shoved her hands deep into her pockets. She felt her heart sink with sadness and her teeth grind with frustration. Even the *eeoo! eeoo! eeoo!* sound made by the jungle birds did not make her feel better.

'I'm sorry, muppet,' her father said. 'I was a bit hard on you just now.'

'You were, Dad,' said Molly. 'We are on the Ring of Fire. This place gets a lot of earthquakes.'

'Okay, muppet. I understand your concern,' her father said. 'But I can't control the behaviour of Earth's tectonic plates, and neither can you, so could you please stop worrying about it?'

Molly knew she probably could not stop worrying about the possibility of an earthquake. But she could find something else to talk about.

'Oh, look, Dad! It's Ted!' she shouted.

The great lizard sauntered across the path in front of them, swishing his tail from side to side. Then he lifted his huge leathery head, looked at Molly and blinked.

'It might be Ted,' her father replied. 'But there's probably lots of those lizards around here.'

'Good point, Dad,' said Molly. 'How would you tell the difference between two of them?'

'There might be some subtle differences in the markings,' her father replied. 'Like human fingerprints, it might be a case of no two are identical.'

Molly thought about the miracle of fingerprints for a moment.

'But do identical twins have identical fingerprints?' she asked.

Her father laughed, then wrapped his arm around her.

'I don't know, muppet,' he said.

'Oh,' said Molly, feeling disappointed.

'There's only one thing I know for sure,' her father said.

'What's that?' Molly asked.

'I know I love you like crazy!' he replied, giving her a squeeze.

'I love you, too, Dad,' she said.

16

HOUSES ON STILTS

Yosia was standing beside the house, next to the stilts.

'What are you doing?' Molly asked.

'Applying a clear varnish,' he replied. 'It helps to keep the wood resilient.'

Molly remembered her parents had always told her that houses require a lot of maintenance. When she was younger, she had thought that was just their excuse for doing boring adult things. But when one of the wooden slats on her balcony had suddenly snapped, she had understood that maintenance was a real thing that had to be done. Underneath her house, she had seen lots of short thick wooden poles called *stumps*. But they had only been a quarter of a meter high, unlike the three-meter gap she was looking at now.

'In Australia we have to spray the wooden stumps under the houses to stop the White Ants from eating them,' she said. 'Are there any wood eating bugs in PNG?'

'Yes,' said Yosia. 'We have the Huhu beetle.'

'Who?' said Molly.

Yosia frowned, then saw the smile on Molly's face.

'Ah. You're a smarty pants,' he said.

Molly knew she was a smarty pants. She also knew that most people found it annoying. But she had some questions for Yosia and she did not want to wait anymore.

'If one of those stilts snapped, we'd be in trouble, wouldn't we?' she asked.

'Yes,' Yosia replied. 'That's why I'm protecting the wood.'

'But if a really big earthquake hit, it wouldn't make much difference, would it?' she asked.

Yosia frowned, so Molly thought she should explain herself.

'We're on the Ring of Fire,' she said. 'That means there is a lot of movement in the tectonic plates, so earthquakes can happen. Also, the mine is close by so—'

'I know what the Ring of Fire is,' said Yosia. 'You don't need to patronize me.'

Molly was not exactly sure what *patronize* meant, but she thought it might have had something to do with speaking to people in a rude manner. Whatever it meant, she saw the deep frown across Yosia's brow, so she knew he was not happy.

'Sorry,' she said. 'I didn't mean anything. I just—'

Suddenly, Molly felt so frustrated, she started to tremble. Her mind was whirling with so many ideas, questions and opinions, all of which seemed to fall out of her mouth at once. She took a few deep breaths, then tried again.

'May I please ask you a question?' she said.

'Of course,' said Yosia.

'Do you worry about earthquakes?' Molly asked.

Yosia put down his paintbrush then stretched his arms up over his head and pointed his fingers to the sky. The brown bird that Molly had seen in the tree next to Yosia's hut flew toward him.

'Hello, my lovely,' he said, lowering his arm.

The bird landed on his forearm, then hopped onto his shoulder and stared at Molly.

'She's a friendly little thing,' said Molly.

'She's my special friend,' Yosia replied. 'Her name is Adali.'

'Pleased to meet you, Adali,' said Molly.

Adali cocked her head to the side, then chirped.

'Wow! It's as though she knows what I'm saying!' said Molly.

Yosia laughed softly, then turned his head to the side. He rubbed his cheek against Adali's brown feathers, and she responded by making a gentle cooing sound.

'Getting back to your question,' said Yosia. 'We don't have a lot of earthquakes down here. When they do come, they're over quickly and they don't do much damage.'

He picked up his paintbrush and continued to paint the stilts.

'When was the last earthquake?' Molly asked.

'Around 2017, I think,' he replied.

'I remember reading about that one,' said Molly. 'It was 7.0 on the Richter scale, but it didn't do much damage because it was shallow. But—'

Molly felt something rough rubbing against her bare leg.

'Ouch,' she said, looking down at Ted. 'Why is he behaving like a cat?'

Yosia smiled.

'Ted has certainly taken a liking to you,' he said. 'Why do you suppose that is?'

Molly shrugged.

'Animals always like me,' she replied. 'It's probably because they know I like them.'

'But you don't like Ted very much,' Yosia argued, moving onto the next stilt.

Molly slumped onto the grass and sighed.

'Oh, Yosia, I miss my cat,' she cried.

'I didn't know you had a cat,' Yosia replied, dipping his brush into the pot of varnish.

'Her name is Kiki, and she is the loveliest thing in the whole universe,' Molly cried. 'My heart is aching for her. Last night was my first night without her and I felt like I was going to die.'

Yosia gave Molly a sad smile.

'I understand,' he said. 'A person's love for an animal can run deep.'

'It sure does,' Molly agreed.

'Maybe you can love Ted, too,' said Yosia.

Molly looked at the large, leathery beast. She did not want to fall in love with him because she would miss him when she went back to Australia.

'Do you like having Adali as your pet?' she asked.

Yosia hesitated.

'She's not so much a pet as a soul mate,' he replied.

'Oh, that's interesting,' said Molly. 'What type of bird is she?'

Yosia hesitated again.

'She's in a class of her own,' he replied. 'One of a kind.'

Molly thought that was a strange answer, but it would have to do for now.

17

UNDER THE MILKY WAY

Molly and Yosia were washing the last of the dinner plates when she heard someone walking up the back steps of her house. Someone appeared at the door. Even through the fly screen, Molly could see it was a pretty woman with long curly grey hair, green eyes and a little dent in the end of her nose.

'Hi, Molly,' she said, smiling.

Molly stared at the woman, wondering who she was.

'Phillipa!' said Molly's mother. 'Please, come in.'

The woman opened the door and stepped inside, offering her hand to Molly. She was pretty, had a nice smile and was very polite, but there was something about her that made Molly feel nervous.

'Hi, Molly,' she said again. 'I'm Michael's mum.'

'Hello, Mrs. Calthorpe,' Molly replied. 'It's very nice to meet you.'

'And you,' said Mrs. Calthorpe.

Molly's mother was at her side, smiling at Mrs. Calthorpe.

'How's Henry?' she asked.

'Ah, the poor thing,' said Mrs. Calthorpe. 'He's out of pain, at least.'

Molly's mother held two tall glasses of clear, bubbling liquid in front of Mrs. Calthorpe.

'Just what the doctor ordered, Phillipa!' she said. 'Something cold and strong for us!'

'Thanks,' said Mrs. Calthorpe. 'After the day I've had, this is just what I need.'

'Trouble in the mine?' Molly's mother asked.

Mrs. Calthorpe sighed, then rubbed her forehead.

'You wouldn't believe the squabbles down there, but I won't spoil our evening complaining about it,' she said. 'It's a lovely night. Shall we sit outside?'

The two mothers made their way down the back steps.

'Shall we sit in the garden too?' Yosia asked.

'Sure,' said Molly.

As she followed Yosia down the back steps, she could think of nothing more than stretching out on the ground and staring at the sky. Michael was already there, doing that very thing, and Adali was sitting on the ground behind his head, staring at him.

'Hello, Adali,' said Molly, kneeling down.

The bird chirped, then hopped onto Yosia's leg.

Molly sat on the picnic blanket beside Michael.

'How's your father?' she asked.

Michael glanced at her.

'He's okay,' he replied. 'As soon as we got to the hospital, they gave him an injection for the pain. By the time Mum arrived, he had a silly smile on his face.'

Molly laughed.

'Are they going to fix his knee?' she asked.

'Yeah, they're going to give him a new knee joint tomorrow afternoon,' he replied.

'Wow! That's brilliant!' said Molly.

She lay on the blanket and looked at the night sky, almost unable to believe what she was seeing. She had to blink a few times to be sure her eyes were working properly. Amidst the deep indigo sky was a mass of golden swirls entwined with a long strip of bright turquoise swirls and some white swirls. And scattered throughout the swirls was a festival of bright stars, glittering like diamonds.

Molly gasped.

'What's happening in the sky?' she asked.

'It's the Milky Way,' said Michael. 'Silly Billy.'

'You're the silly one,' Molly said. 'We live *inside* the Milky Way, which means we can't see it.'

Michael's head scratched against the blanket as he turned to look at Molly. Across his brow was a deep frown, and his mouth had shrunk to a tiny round hole.

'Are you being funny?' he asked.

'No,' Molly replied.

'The Milky Way is huge!' he said.

'I know that!' Molly snapped.

'We only occupy a tiny part of it, which means we can sometimes see the rest of it,' Michael explained. 'It's called astronomy, girl. Look into it.'

'Are you being rude to me?' said Molly. 'Just because you're two years older than me doesn't mean you can be rude to me.'

The boy scoffed, then rubbed his eyes.

'Whatever,' he said.

'Be nice, Michael,' said Mrs. Calthorpe.

'I *am* being nice,' Michael whined.

But Michael was not being nice. He was being rude and grumpy because he'd had a bad day. Watching his father's enormous body collapse like a house of cards could not have been pleasant, Molly imagined. Then watching him get hauled onto a monster truck and tied to the railing must have been awful. She knew if that had been her father, she would have cried non-stop.

'Gosh, it's lovely,' said Mrs. Calthorpe, staring at the sky.

Molly's mother looked up, too.

Her mane of glossy brown hair cascaded down the back of her chair.

'Oh, wow!' she said.

'Have you ever seen the sky like this before, Mum?' Molly asked.

'Only once, when I was about your age,' she replied. 'I spent a lot of time in the garden back then. During the summer, my sister and I would sleep in a tent among the eucalyptus trees. Not that we got much sleep, with the cicadas screeching all night.'

Michael laughed.

'Those things sound really funny,' he said.

'They sure do,' said Molly's mother. 'We were always so tired in the morning, the only thing that got us out of bed was knowing that we'd get to play with the fairies down by the creek.'

Molly felt so excited, she sat up.

'Do you still see fairies, Mum?' she asked.

Her mother frowned, then burst out laughing.

'Of course not!' she said.

Mrs. Calthorpe laughed, too.

Molly did not like being laughed at. It hurt her feelings.

'Gardens are great,' said Mrs. Calthorpe. 'I loved my veggie patch back home.'

Molly remembered her veggie patch in her garden in Australia. The tomatoes had always been the easiest to grow because of the heat and bright sunshine. But her favorite things had been the cosmos flowers. Kiki had liked them, too. She would press her little pink nose against the petals, then step back and twitch her nose from side to side as though thinking about their scent. Then she would do it again.

'Ow!' said Molly's mother, slapping her arm.

'What's wrong, Mum?' Molly asked.

'The mosquitoes!' her mother replied. 'They're vicious tonight.'

Molly glanced at the round yellow citronella candle hanging from the clotheslines in a loose net. About the size of a volleyball, it produced a strong lemony scent that she had always loved.

'I've just been bitten, too,' said Mrs. Calthorpe, slapping her leg.

Adali swooped over to Mrs. Calthorpe and pecked at something near her other leg.

'Hey! That little birdie just ate a mosquito!' said Mrs. Calthorpe.

Molly felt certain Adali could understand everything that everyone was saying.

'Let's go inside,' her mother said, standing up.

Molly gazed at the sky again.

'Why haven't I seen this before?' she asked.

'You need a clear sky with no clouds, no moon or other light pollution,' Yosia replied.

Molly looked for the moon.

'You're right,' she said. 'There's no moon tonight.'

'Of course there's a moon,' Michael snarled. 'It's just really small and it's on the opposite side of the sky tonight.'

'I get it,' said Molly. 'Please don't patronize me.'

Michael groaned.

'I didn't mean to,' he said. 'I'm just tired, and worried about Dad.'

'I know,' said Molly.

She glanced at Yosia.

'Do you think anyone lives up there?' she asked.

'It's hard to know,' Yosia replied. 'But, with billions of stars in our Milky Way, it seems unlikely that we'd be the only intelligent life in the neighborhood.'

'Do you have any cool stories about how the stars were born?' Molly asked.

'My stories are the same as yours,' Yosia replied. 'I learned the same things at school that you and Michael are learning now. Except there was no Hubble Telescope during my school days. You kids are lucky to have access to so much knowledge.'

Molly felt something moving her hair, so she sat up and looked behind her. There was Ted, pushing the side of his enormous belly into the place where Molly's head had been resting.

'He seems to be offering himself as a pillow,' said Yosia, laughing.

Molly did not feel good about using an animal as a pillow, least of all a giant lizard, but she was learning that this creature was different. For some reason, he wanted to be close to her, so she lowered her head onto his body. As the back of her scalp made contact with his leathery skin, and her neck was cradled by his belly, Molly realized there could be worse things in life than using a lizard as a pillow. And Ted, it seemed, was happy because he flopped onto his belly and groaned like a dog that is being scratched in exactly the right place.

'Yosia, you seem to know about science and magic,' said Molly. 'Which do you believe in?'

'Both,' Yosia replied.

'Both?' Molly echoed. 'How does that work?'

'I think I'd like to hear the answer to this, too,' Michael said.

'Okay,' said Yosia. '*Magic* is the word we use for something we don't understand, and *science* is the word we use for something we've learned to understand.'

Michael sat up and stared at Yosia.

'So, what did you do to *me*?' he asked. 'Was that magic or science?'

'I didn't do anything to you, Michael,' said Yosia. 'Your lack of power in that moment was a side effect of the adjustment I made to space-time. Molly couldn't move, either.'

'Oh!' said Molly. 'I didn't know that.'

'What did you just say about space-time?' Michael asked.

'There was one reality in which the butterflies were dead,' Yosia explained. 'Do you agree?'

'Yes,' said Michael. 'I killed them.'

Yosia nodded.

'There was another reality in which the butterflies were alive,' he continued. 'I brought those two realities together. To do that, I had to adjust space-time.'

'What the heck does that mean?' Michael demanded.

Yosia sat up and looked at Michael.

'We live in a reality in which time only moves in one direction - from the past to the future. Do you agree?' he asked.

'Yes,' said Michael.

'In some realities, the future can change the past,' Yosia explained. 'And in other realities, everything is happening all at once. There are an infinite number of realities, each as different as the next.'

'Are you talking about the multiverse theory?' Michael asked.

'Precisely!' said Yosia. 'All I did was bring together two separate realities.'

Michael sat up further.

'You must know how strange that sounds,' he said.

'Not to me,' said Molly.

'But did you hear him, Molly?' said Michael. 'He just said he brought two different realities together! Have you ever met anyone who says they can do that?'

Molly knew she had heard these ideas before, but—

'No,' she replied.

Molly lifted her head from Ted's body and looked at Yosia. He was lying down again, staring up at the sky with his twinkling black eyes. Adali was asleep on his chest, her little beak buried in his curly black hair.

'Can you teach us how to do that?' she asked.

'No,' Yosia replied. 'In fact, I rarely allow people to see me do such things.'

'Why did you let us see?' Molly asked.

Yosia sighed, then rubbed his eyes.

'Considering the number of creatures that had lost their lives, it felt urgent and necessary that I intervene,' he said. 'Also, I sensed extreme distress from you, Molly.'

'How did you know I was distressed?' Molly asked. 'And how did you know where to find me?'

Yosia laughed, then shook his head.

'It's no mystery, Molly,' he replied. 'I heard you shouting at Michael, then I saw you stomp up the steps after him. I knew conflict would ensue.'

Michael scoffed.

'Conflict certainly did ensue,' he said.

But Molly did not regret her actions. Not for a moment.

18

HOUSE HELPERS

Molly sat in Michael's back garden. It was like hers, but not as nice. And there was a hut down at the bottom of the garden, but not as nice as Yosia's hut.

'Does anyone live in there?' she asked, pointing at it.

'No,' Michael replied. 'Before we came here, Dad said he didn't want a house helper.'

'Why?' Molly asked.

'He thinks it's wrong,' Michael replied.

'Why?'

'Dad said this country belongs to the locals, so they should not have to work for the Australian and American families,' Michael replied.

Molly could understand why Mr. Calthorpe would feel that way. And it made her wonder about Yosia. Was he happy, working a house helper for her family, she wondered?

'I often wonder who lived in that hut before we arrived,' said Michael.

'We can ask Yosia some time,' Molly said.

A smirk crept up Michael's face.

'Yosia might tell us he manipulated space-time and made them vanish,' he said.

Molly scoffed at Michael's joke, which made him smile.

'I feel bad, though, because it means someone is out of a job,' he said.

Molly did not understand much about jobs. She knew her father had a job as a mining engineer. And she knew her mother once had a job as a professor of anthropology. But she did not understand why people had jobs. She thought it would be much better if everyone was free to read and learn and go on adventures and help each other whenever they can.

She glanced at Ted, lazing under the sun.

'He doesn't have a job,' she said, pointing at the lizard.

She felt restless and in need of another adventure. She remembered that the inactive volcano had been on her list of things to see since she had arrived in PNG. And it was just on the far side of the plantation, which was only a few meters from where she and Michael were sitting, so it seemed a shame to miss the opportunity.

'Let's go for a walk,' she said.

'Where to?' Michael asked.

'That way,' said Molly, pointing at the trees behind the hut.

Michael shrugged.

'Okay,' he said. 'But don't blame me if you get hit on the head by a coconut.'

Molly laughed, then tapped Ted on the belly. The great beast rolled onto his stumpy legs and pointed his nose toward the end of the garden.

'Do all the animals in this place understand what we're saying?' she asked.

'I think so,' Michael replied. 'And it makes me feel I might be losing my mind.'

'Speaking of which,' said Molly. 'We need water before he head out.'

'Good point,' Michael said. 'I'll fill some bottles. Back in a sec!'

Molly watched her new friend gallop toward the back steps of his house. She felt good about their friendship. The boy had kept his word - to do no harm to any creature - and he was fun to be with.

19

CROSSING THE PLANTATION

Behind the hut, Molly stared at a ragged collection of shrubs and trees.

'I guess we have to punch our way through,' she sighed.

'Yep,' said Michael. 'I'll go first.'

Molly followed her big friend, grateful that he remembered to hold the branches away from her, instead of letting them flick back into her face.

When they reached the far side of the thicket, she saw several rows of crop. The dark green leaves were folded and there was a tiny yellow dot in the center.

'Corn,' she said.

'Yep,' said Michael.

Although the rows seemed to go on forever, there were only a few. And on either side was a wild and thick jungle. Molly found the view both beautiful and interesting, unlike anything she had ever seen before.

'I don't really understand what I'm looking at,' she said.

'It's called agroforestry,' said Michael.

'What's that?' Molly asked.

'They're trying to let go of the traditional monoculture and—'

'What's monoculture?' Molly asked.

'It's when there's only one thing growing in the ground,' Michael replied.

'Oh, yeah, I've seen that,' said Molly.

'I'd be surprised if you hadn't,' Michael replied. 'It's been standard farming practice for hundreds of years, but it's really bad for the soil and it offers a smorgasbord of munchies to pests.'

'Smorgasbord,' Molly giggled.

'This approach, with everything mixed in together, solves those problems,' Michael explained.

'It looks nicer, too,' said Molly. 'I can see the yam and sweet potato crops over there, and some pineapple bushes mixed in between. And I can see some banana trees and coconut trees and—Oh! Is that a Bird of Paradise?'

Michael spun around and looked up, but he was too late. The bird with the long orange and white tail feathers had already disappeared among the leaves of a huge tree.

'Never mind,' said Molly. 'Let's just follow this path.'

The dirt path between the rows of corn was narrow, but flat enough to walk along. Ted raced ahead, swishing his wide body from side to side, knocking the corn around.

'Those moving crops would look scary to anyone who didn't know Ted,' she said.

'Yeah,' Michael laughed. 'It would look like a bad horror movie.'

'I wouldn't know,' said Molly. 'I'm not allowed to watch horror movies.'

'You're better off without them,' Michael said.

Molly was enjoying the walk. But the magic and mystery of the surrounding jungle was calling her, and she wondered what it would feel like to run through the wilderness with her arms open wide.

'Hey,' Michael whispered.

Molly looked at him, pointing to a huge, pale grey branch. There were a lot of leaves around it and a giant palm frond was partly covering it. But soon, she realized Michael was pointing to a chocolate brown and golden tree kangaroo. Its pale blue eyes were staring at her and its round pink nose was moving slightly, breathing in her scent.

'Aww, that's *so* cute,' she whispered.

Then she saw a baby peering out from the safety of its mother's pouch.

'Aww, there's a baby,' she cooed.

Michael laughed gently.

'Cute,' all right,' he said.

When Molly returned to the path, she noticed Ted, half turned around in the middle of the path. His head had snapped some corn cobs on one side of the path and his tail had snapped several on the other side. As Molly stepped toward him, he lifted his face and looked at her. The sun lit up his warm brown eyes, and he blinked slowly. So slowly, Molly saw his internal eyelids close before his external lids closed.

'Wow, that was weird,' said Michael.

Molly laughed.

'Didn't you know they have two sets of eyelids?' she asked.

'Yeah, but I've never seen a lizard behave in that

dreamy kind of way,' Michael replied. 'Honestly, Molly, I think Ted thinks he's your pet cat. Or dog. I'm not sure which.'

Molly felt her heart swell as she recalled the furry black face of her cat, Kiki. For a moment, she felt a tightening in the back of her throat, like she was about to cry. But somehow, she was able to shake it off and feel excited about the adventure ahead.

'Okay, Ted. Lead on,' she said.

The great, leathery beast turned around and continued along the dirt path.

As the jungle thickened, Molly found herself surrounded by an orchestra of bird sounds. Their performance - which included *eeoo! eeoo!* and *woochoo!* and *arck!* and *beerk!* - soon had her laughing out loud.

'They're hilarious!' she said.

Michael laughed, too.

'They're nature's comedians, that's for sure!' he said.

Molly noticed a small collection of huts. They were all built on stilts that were as high as the ones under her own house. The bases were simple square shapes. The walls and roofs were made from the dried fronds of palm trees. And a thin wooden ladder rested at the entrance of each hut, which made Molly think of all the times she had climbed up to the top bunk bed during school camps.

'Are we allowed to be here?' she whispered, noticing several people working in their gardens.

'Yeah, I think so,' Michael replied. 'It's a thoroughfare.'

Then he smiled, waved and said 'hello'. The people returned the greeting but kept to their gardening. Molly liked the way the vegetable gardens and fruit trees were scattered between the trees and huts. It was a view that felt like a feast for her eyes.

She also liked the look of the people. One woman was squatting down, picking some of the vegetables. Another was stripping the dead brown leaves from a banana tree. A young man was raking the ground at the base of the huts. Someone else was picking oval-shaped fruits from a tree and another person was using a knife to strip the bark from a young tree.

No one seemed concerned about her and Michael wandering through their village. Nor were they interested in what she, Michael and Ted might have been up to. That made Molly feel that the road ahead must have been well travelled and safe.

But when the jungle became so thick that she could no longer see the path, she felt they might have taken a wrong turn. She rummaged through Michael's backpack, found a bottle, and took a long drink before returning it.

'Looks like we need to hack through again,' said Michael. 'Follow me.'

20

ONE SMALL STEP

Almost an hour later, Molly took her first step onto the red-brown rock at the base of the volcano. Looking up, she figured it would have been about two hundred meters high, and there was not a single tree or shrub in sight.

'I feel like I've just landed on Mars,' she said.

'Yeah,' Michael laughed.

Molly could not understand what she was looking at.

'It seems strange,' she said. 'I mean, this volcano has been inactive for years, so there should be *something* growing here.'

'Agreed,' said Michael. 'There's enough cracks in the rocks for something to have sprouted up.'

'Especially as the area is completely surrounded by jungle and crops,' Molly added.

A great billow of white gas shot up from the volcano. Molly blinked a few times, and put her handkerchief over her mouth and nose, but the cloud vanished in an instant, leaving no scent in the air.

'That was weird,' said Michael, taking his hands away

from his face. 'It makes me wonder what's down there. Are you curious, too?'

'Heck, yeah!' Molly replied. 'Let's go!'

After the first few steps up the side of the volcano, Molly wondered if anyone else had walked this way in recent times. But it was difficult to tell because the rock was so solid, there were no footprints or tire tracks.

'I reckon I'll be dreaming about red rock tonight,' said Michael.

The air felt warm and dry. They were walking in the shadow of the volcano and Molly was looking forward to reaching the sunny top. Ted would be happier there, too, she knew. But for now, the beast seemed content to canter alongside her like a faithful canine.

'I'd love to know if Ted's been here before,' she said.

'If someone had strapped a camera to his head, we could watch the movie,' said Michael.

Molly laughed, imagining how boring that movie would be - rocks for a few minutes, followed by hours of absolutely nothing while Ted lay flat, sunning himself.

21

ON TOP OF THE VOLCANO

It was bright and sunny on top of the volcano. Molly felt it warming her bones. She gazed at the golden-red and pinkish-red rock all around her, feeling like a true explorer. This, she knew, was the fire in the belly of all explorers - to explore a place simply because it exists. She stretched her arms up high, threw back her head and stared at the vibrant blue sky.

'You should really see this,' Michael called out.

He was looking down at the bottom of the volcano, so Molly did the same.

'Wow!' she said. 'I wasn't expecting anything like this!'

Directly below her was a round patch of something bright blue. Beyond that, the ground descended into a luscious green haven that seemed to stretch on for a kilometer.

'It looks like a tropical rainforest!' she said.

'It sure does,' said Michael.

'But we're standing on a barren volcano, without a

single shrub or blade of grass in sight,' said Molly. 'How can there possibly be a jungle below?'

'It's weird, all right,' said Michael. 'What do you make of that patch of blue directly below?'

Molly felt she was looking at something familiar, but she did not know what.

'What is it?' she asked.

'It's hard to say for sure,' Michael replied. 'But it looks very similar to the bright blue lake we saw yesterday inside the cave in the mine.'

Instantly, Molly knew Michael was right. It was exactly the same blue-green color as the lake in the cave. She took a long drink of water, then returned the bottle to Michael's backpack.

'There *must* be an underground channel connecting them,' she said.

'I reckon so, too,' said Michael. 'The question is - why would anyone want to connect them?'

'It might not be deliberate,' Molly argued. 'It could be one of those natural connections. You know, one of those, um, what are they called?'

'A subterranean strait?' said Michael.

'That's it!' Molly said. 'The owners of the mine might not even know that their sulfuric acid and copper sulphate lake is leaching underground and finding its way to the surface over here.'

'Well, someone knows,' said Michael, pointing to a spot just inside the mouth of the volcano.

It was about five meters away from where they stood.

'Is that a handle?' Molly asked.

As Michael nodded, Molly realized it was the first of many handles on a ladder.

'So, if we climb down there, we'll be able to walk around the edge of the lake, then jump down to that little stone path that goes down to the jungle,' she said.

'My thoughts, exactly!' said Michael. 'Are you ready for an adventure?'

'Let's go!' said Molly.

22

DEEP INSIDE THE VOLCANO

Ted bolted down the internal wall of the volcano, headfirst.

'Look at him go!' Molly shouted.

She imagined the lizard's claws must have been digging into the rock face and his long muscular tail pressing against the wall above him, to stop him from falling.

'There's no stopping that guy,' said Michael. 'I just hope he avoids that lake.'

'He will,' Molly said. 'He's been here before. I'm sure of it.'

Within minutes of the descent, Molly's hands were starting to ache. The steel handles, designed for adults, were so thick she had to stretch every muscle and joint in her fingers just to wrap around them. And she had to grip them, to stop herself from falling. It felt awkward and painful, but she could not give up because giving up would have meant falling down.

'I'm not landing in that toxic lake!' she shouted.

'No, you're not!' Michael shouted. 'Just keep your eyes on your hands.'

By the time they reached the bottom, Molly's hands were throbbing.

'I don't fancy doing that again,' she said, staring at her palms.

Covered in red welts, she knew they would hurt even more the next day. And the pads at the base of each finger had turned yellow, preparing to form callouses.

'Ouch,' said Michael, staring at her palms.

He shuffled sideways around the lake, and Molly followed him, pressing her back hard against the rock wall. The diameter of the lake was about six meters, so she figured it would not take long to sidle halfway around it. Then she would reach the place where the wall bulged outward and away from the lake.

In the meantime, she was terrified of falling in face first. She could not think of anything worse than that. At least, not until she looked at Michael. Beads of sweat were erupting from his entire face and neck as he struggled to keep away from the edge of the lake. But it was difficult, Molly could tell, because his feet were so long they protruded over the edge of the ledge. She was terrified he might fall in, but she did not dare say so.

Another white cloud shot up from the center of the lake. It was just as thick and fast-moving as the last one had been. Molly turned her face away, but it dissipated in seconds, leaving no scent or change in the air quality.

'Geez,' said Michael, gasping.

'It's very weird,' Molly said.

Soon, her fingertips caressed the part of the volcano wall that bulged outward, and she exhaled a loud sigh of relief. Michael, a step of ahead of her, jumped off the ledge and landed on the stone path. With nothing behind him but open air, and the surprising jungle, he held out his hand.

'Thanks,' said Molly, taking his hand. 'I was terrified of falling in.'

'Yeah, that's the thing about danger,' Michael said. 'The more you think about the worst thing happening, the more you are likely to make it happen.'

As Molly took her first step onto the stone path, she noticed the surrounding grass was just as green as it had appeared from the top of the volcano. But when she bent down and stared at it up close, she could see the base of every blade was the same bright turquoise color as the lake.

'That is *so* weird,' she said.

'Yes, I think we can agree that *weird* is the word for the day,' said Michael.

Molly followed him down the path through a cluster of shrubs that were about as high as her ankles. Their leaves were bright purple and heart-shaped.

'I've never seen anything like these,' she said.

'Me neither,' said Michael.

Molly was tempted to touch one of the leaves, but something told her it would not be wise to touch anything she could not identify. So she leaned in and stared at it, surprised to notice the veins were the same bright turquoise color as the lake.

'Hey, th—' she started.

She saw Michael, about a meter down the path, as rigid as stone.

'What's wrong?' she whispered.

Michael lifted his hand and signaled for Molly to come

closer. She approached him, and followed his line of vision, but could not see the problem.

'What's wrong?' she asked, again.

Michael brought his hand forward and pointed between the leaves. Then Molly saw it. About the size of her fist, and a brown-green color, was an eyeball. At its center was a long, thin black stripe. The pupil of a reptile. She felt frozen with terror, unable to look away. The eye did not look away, either. Slowly, Molly took a step back, but the eye did not move. Then she stepped sideways. Still, the eye did not move.

'Is it dead?' she whispered.

Michael waved his hand in front of the eye, but it did not move.

'What's it doing?' Molly whispered.

Michael relaxed his body, then laughed out loud.

'It's not an eye!' he said.

'What is it?' Molly asked.

Without answering, Michael leaned forward and grabbed it.

'No!' Molly squealed.

A moment later, she was staring at the thing in Michael's hand. She could see the black center that had looked like a reptilian pupil was actually the center of a flower. And the brown-green ball that had appeared to be an iris was a cluster of tightly packed petals.

'Isn't this amazing?' said Michael, peeling the petals away from the center.

Molly could feel her heart slowing to a normal pace, but she was still shaken by the experience.

'What kind of flower dresses up like that?' she snapped.

'I don't know,' Michael replied. 'But where there's one, there's bound to be more.'

Now that Molly was alert to the eyeball flowers, she saw them everywhere. There was something else, too. It had thick straight stems, like those of a lily. And the head was a white flower that curled at the edges, just like a lily. But unlike a lily, this white flower looked as though it had been attacked with a bright turquoise pen. The scribbles reminded Molly of the first drawing she had done at the age of two years.

'Those bright turquoise squiggles are no coincidence, are they?' she said.

Michael shook his head.

'Nope. These plants are being fed by that lake,' he replied.

'Which is weird, because the lake is full of sulfuric acid and copper sulfate,' said Molly.

She gazed at the vast jungle in the distance.

'Do you want to know what I reckon?' she said.

'What?' said Michael.

'This whole place is one big experiment,' Molly said.

Michael looked at her for a moment, his eyes exploring each of hers. Then he nodded.

'The question is - *whose* experiment?' he asked.

Molly gazed up at the top of the volcano.

'Do you want to leave?' Michael asked.

Molly thought about it for a moment. On the one hand, she wanted to run back home and tell Yosia about everything they had seen in this strange place. But on the other hand, she wanted to stay and explore. Eventually she decided that a science experiment would probably be a safe place.

'I'd like to stay for a while,' she said.

Michael glanced at her again.

'Okay,' he said slowly. 'Just a bit longer.'

He continued down the stone path.

Molly wondered where Ted was, which made her laugh.

'What's so funny?' Michael asked.

'Oh, that silly lizard,' she replied. 'I'm becoming too attached to him.'

Michael laughed, too.

'The feeling seems to be mutual,' he said, pointing down the path. 'He's waiting for you.'

Molly saw Ted's head protruding from the shrubs. The rest of him, she knew, would be nestled among the eyeball flowers, the purple heart-shaped leaves, the turquoise squiggled lilies and whatever else might be growing in there. She laughed at the sight of the ugly beast surrounded by flowers.

'He's probably enjoying the warmer, wetter air down here,' she said.

Then she noticed something else about the air. It was still and silent.

'Hey, Michael, I haven't heard a single bird,' she said. 'Have you?'

'Not a chirp,' he replied.

He continued down the path through some taller shrubs that were about as high as his shoulders. As Molly followed, she noticed the stone path was becoming closed in by the larger foliage. She also noticed the eyeball flower was growing from a vine that was hanging from the branches of another strange shrub with curly red fingers where leaves would normally be. Among the red-fingered shrubs were some taller trees. They were identical in shape to the banana tree. But their leaves were bright yellow with a turquoise vein running down their center.

'This is getting too weird,' she said.

'Strange plants probably mean strange animals,' said Michael. 'I think we should turn back.'

'Agreed,' said Molly. 'If the plants were tiny, we could assume—'

Molly did not get to finish what she was saying before a loud *whack!* got her attention. She looked in the direction of the sound and saw the shrubs moving. Something grey and shiny was darting around. At first she thought it was Ted, but then she saw him racing after the thing. Next she saw Ted's tail flick into the air, and a moment after that, she heard a loud crunch.

'Ted's caught something,' Michael whispered.

Ted returned to the path, holding something between his jaws. Whatever it was, Molly could tell it was still alive because it was wriggling. It was shiny and hairless, like a reptile. But its back legs were shaped like a kangaroo's and its front legs were tiny.

'It looks like a dinosaur!' she shrieked.

'It *is* a dinosaur!' said Michael.

Ted's massive jaws bit through the creature's neck, severing its head from its body. As the head fell to the ground, Molly noticed it was grey and leathery, just like a lizard. Its eyes were brown with long black pupils, just like

DEEP INSIDE THE VOLCANO 105

a lizard. But on top of the head was a large, round bone. And instead of a mouth, it had a sharply curved beak.

'That ... does ... not ... exist,' she stammered.

'No, it does not,' Michael agreed. 'Molly, we need to go!'

Molly heard the sound of branches breaking and foliage being torn apart. Then she heard a low-pitched cry that sounded like a whale calling to its family across thousands of kilometers. She stared down the path and saw several trees falling aside. Between them was something large, round and grey.

'Now, Molly!' Michael shouted.

But Molly could not move. Something emerged from between the trees. It looked like a rhinoceros. Two horns protruded from its nose, exactly where rhinoceros horns would be, and an extra horn grew from each side of its mouth. Strangest of all was the fan-shaped bone growing from the back of its neck. It was bounding up the path, straight toward Molly, shaking the ground with every step.

'Run!' Michael screamed.

Molly was about to run, but what happened next kept her there, staring in disbelief. Ted leapt onto the path in front of the beast. He stood on his back legs, making himself almost two meters tall. He lifted his front legs, spread his claws, then hissed so loudly, Molly had to put her hands over her ears.

'Run!' Michael shouted again.

As Molly ran up the path, she could hear the awful sound of reptilian conflict behind her, rattling every bone in her body. Soon, she was running across the grass, her eyes fixed on the ladder she would climb. A moment later, she leapt up to the ledge around the lake. Michael threw his arm in front of her, pinning her to the wall.

'Thanks,' she gasped.

'Ready to climb?' he asked.

Molly could see her leathery friend emerging from the shrubs.

'Wait for Ted!' she shouted.

The beast scuttled up the path. Molly could see he was not bleeding, nor was he missing any limbs. He ran just as fast and comically as he usually did. She guessed he must have won the fight with the rhinoceros-type creature. Or perhaps he had just run from it. Either way, Molly knew Ted had saved her life.

'Come on, Ted!' she called out.

Michael clutched the first handle on the rock wall.

'We need to go,' he said.

'Just a second,' said Molly.

Ted leapt up to the ledge.

'Yes!' Molly squealed.

She imagined it was a move Ted had made many times before, so she was shocked when he lost his grip on the ledge and slipped. Then, for one awful moment that seemed to last forever, she saw him slide into the lake.

'No!' she shrieked.

She leaned forward, ready to grab Ted's tail or claw or head, whichever part of him surfaced first, but Michael held her back.

'Steady!' he shouted, griping her arm.

Molly stared at the lake, waiting for Ted to emerge. But there was no movement in the water. It had returned to its still state as though absolutely nothing had happened.

She started to cry.

Michael gripped her wrist and brought her hand to the first handle in the ladder.

'Climb!' she said.

As Molly's aching hands stretched around the first handle, she started to sob. And she did not stop until she reached the top of the volcano.

23

A REALLY BIG FLYING THING

When she reached the top, Molly lay on her side and curled into a tight ball. She felt as though she had cried an ocean of tears and her eyes were so exhausted, she closed them. Michael flopped onto the rock beside her.

'Poor Ted,' he gasped.

'I can't believe it,' said Molly.

She rolled onto her belly and stared at the lake below.

'I can't believe it,' she said again. 'Ted would know how to swim. Why didn't he surface?'

Michael sighed.

'I have a theory, but I don't think you'll like it,' he said.

Molly had her own theories, and she had been churning through them during the climb up the volcano wall. Her first theory was that the lake was far deeper than she and Michael had imagined, and it was home to a great water monster that had dragged Ted under. Her second theory was that there was a strange gravitational pull in the subterranean strait that connected this lake to the one in the cave. But Michael, she knew, would have different ideas.

'Okay, tell me your theory,' she said.

'I wouldn't mind betting that the lake is more acidic than we thought,' said Michael.

'What's your point?' Molly asked.

Michael rolled onto his side and stared at her.

'Like those lakes in Tanzania that burn any animal that drinks from them—' he started.

Molly groaned.

'Those lakes are highly alkaline,' she said. 'This one is acid.'

Michael's face fell.

'Sorry, I didn't mean to be rude,' said Molly. 'I'm just really upset.'

Michael flopped onto his back again and closed his eyes.

'I understand,' he said.

As Molly watched the sun skim the surface of Michael's face and neck, she thought about Ted, knowing he would have enjoyed lazing beside them. She stared at the lake again, but there was still no movement. Then she stared at the stone path, following it through the grass and shrubs they had visited.

Further down the hill, much further than she and Michael had walked, Molly could see the treetops moving. At first that did not seem strange to her, because a gentle breeze or a flock of birds could easily cause that type of movement. Then she remembered she had felt no breeze and heard no birds when she had been down there. More importantly, she knew, if she could see the treetops moving from this distance, something very large had to be moving them. A moment later, something absolutely massive rose into the sky.

'What's that?' she shouted.

'Hm?' said Michael, almost asleep.

'That!' Molly screamed.

Michael sat up and stared in the direction Molly was pointing. His bottom lip trembled.

'It's a ... Really. Big. Flying. Thing,' he said.

Molly leapt to her feet.

'Get down!' Michael hissed, pulling her leg.

Molly lay down again and stared at the creature. It was a deep brown color, a stark contrast against the blue sky, and it was flying straight toward them.

'It's a bat,' she said.

'Bat wings aren't twenty meters across!' Michael hissed. 'Keep your head down!'

Molly looked down at the lake.

'There's something moving down there, too,' she said.

A dark shape spiraled upward, broke through the surface of the lake, then pulled itself out.

'It's Ted!' Molly shouted.

'Shh!' Michael hissed.

Molly watched Ted commence the climb up the wall. He was not as confident, powerful or fast as before, but he still had all four legs and his long tail was intact.

'Come on, Ted,' she whispered.

The flying creature turned and stared at Ted.

'Oh, no,' Molly whined, staring at the raptor.

Its head looked like a plain, round ball. From the top grew a long bone that curved over the back of its body and finished at a sharp point. And from the bottom grew a long and sharply pointed beak which, Molly knew, would be full of teeth. The monster threw back its head and screeched, making a sound unlike anything she had ever heard before.

'It's going straight toward Ted!' she cried.

'I know,' said Michael. 'So once it locks onto him, we can make a run for it!'

'What?' said Molly. 'How could you say—'

'Would you prefer the monster to eat *you*?' Michael asked.

Molly could see the raptor's body was about the same size as Michael's. And its wingspan would have been at least twenty meters across. At the centre of each wing was a tiny claw which it would use to hold its prey still while it ripped them apart with its beak.

'Oh, Ted,' she cried.

Ted continued to scramble up the wall, but the awful creature closed around him.

'I can't watch,' said Molly, burying her face in her hands.

But when Ted hissed loudly, she looked again. The raptor hovered over Ted, its massive wings making a *voompf! voompf!* sound.

'Please don't hurt him,' Molly whispered.

The monster titled its head back and aimed the tip of its sharp beak at Ted's neck. Then it brought its head forward, ready to pierce him. But Ted had other ideas. He unlatched one of his claws and swung away, avoiding contact. He left the wall exposed, so when the monster brought its head forward, its beak smashed into the rock.

'Yes!' Molly squealed.

The raptor struggled for several moments to free its beak from the wall. By the time it did, it seemed to have lost the will to live because it collapsed its wings and plummeted toward the lake. Then it slid through the surface like a hot knife through butter, without making a splash. And its long, thin tail, like that of a stingray, followed a second later.

'Awesome!' Michael screamed, punching the air with his fist.

'Ted!' Molly called out again, crawling to the mouth of the volcano.

A few moments later, Ted's head appeared above the mouth of the volcano. His eyes were closed, his mouth was open, and his tongue was hanging out.

'Good boy!' said Molly, placing her hand under one of his front legs.

Michael held the other and together, they pulled their leathery friend out of the volcano.

'Oh, thank goodness,' said Molly, wrapping her arm around the lizard's body.

But he was shaking so much, he could not even bend his legs to lie on his belly.

'What's happening to him?' Molly cried.

'Dunno,' said Michael. 'But I'm going to carry him home.'

He slid his hands under Ted's belly, then lifted. By the time he stood up, the lizard's body had gone completely floppy - his head hung over one of Michael's arms and his tail hung over the other.

'I think he's dying,' Molly cried.

'Nope, I can feel his heart beating,' said Michael. 'He's just conserving energy.'

Molly hoped the boy was right.

24

WALKING HOME

During the walk back through the jungle, Molly listened to Michael grunting as he struggled to carry Ted. She felt bad that all she could do to help was hold Ted's tail and stop it from dragging along the ground. More than anything, she felt pleased she had made friends with Michael. Not only had he kept his promise - to do no harm to any creature - but now he was doing everything in his power to save this one's life.

As they approached the group of huts they had seen before, Molly noticed several people dropping their gardening tools and staring. She knew it would have been a strange sight - a boy and a girl carrying a lizard home. And perhaps her face was red from crying, but she was determined to be friendly.

'Hello,' she said, smiling and nodding.

A young man, slightly bigger than Michael, stepped forward.

'Let me help,' he said.

Michael groaned with relief.

'Thanks, mate,' he said. 'He's heavier than he looks.'

As the young man slid his arms under Ted's body, his firm and bulging arm muscles soon buckled under the weight of the sleeping lizard.

'I see what you mean,' he laughed.

Michael's arms dropped by his sides as he groaned with relief.

'You did really well to carry him this far,' said Molly.

'This poor creature needs warmth and rest,' said the young man.

'Would you mind carrying him to my place? It's just over there,' said Molly, pointing.

'Sure,' the man replied. 'Yosia will know what to do.'

Molly did not know how the young man knew she lived at Yosia's place, but now was not the time to ask silly questions. She was just grateful for his help.

25

YOSIA KNOWS GIDEON

Yosia was in the garden, painting more varnish on the wooden stilts under the house.

'Oh, thank goodness, Yosia. You're here!' Molly cried.

Yosia dropped his paintbrush and ran toward them.

'Gideon!' he said to the young man.

'Yosia, it's good to see you,' Gideon replied.

He carried Ted to a sunny patch in the garden and laid him on the grass.

'What happened?' Yosia asked.

Molly looked at Michael, wondering how to answer the question. She did not want to say anything in front of someone she did not know, and she could see Michael was not going to, either. She slumped onto the grass beside Ted and wrapped her fingers around his tail, trying not to cry. Yosia ran his hands down Ted's torso, but the lizard remained flat and unmoving and his eyes were still firmly closed.

'I just can't believe it,' Molly cried.

'I think he'll be okay,' said Yosia.

Then he looked up at Gideon.

'Thanks, buddy,' he said. 'I'd like to visit you tomorrow if that's okay.'

Gideon nodded, then stepped back.

'See you then,' he said.

Michael, who was somehow still standing, offered his hand to Gideon.

'Thanks again, Gideon,' he said. 'I'm Michael, by the way.'

'No problem, Michael,' said Gideon. 'See you sometime.'

Molly waved goodbye. Gideon returned the gesture with a nod, and then he left.

'We need a blanket,' said Yosia. 'Do either of you have a spare?'

Michael ran to the piles of junk under Molly's house. As she watched him rummage around, she hoped he would not be attacked by any spiders like the large and horrible one that had chased her the day she had arrived. But he returned a moment later with an old blanket in hand.

'Good,' said Yosia, smoothing the blanket over Ted's body.

Then he looked at Molly and Michael.

'Okay, it's just the three of us,' he said. 'Tell me what happened.'

26

YOSIA WANTS ANSWERS

Michael groaned, then sprawled across the grass. Just seeing him do that made Molly aware of the wave of exhaustion flowing through her own body. She lay down, too, with her head in the shade. For a moment, she could do no more than pull a bottle from Michael's backpack and drink. When her mouth finally felt moist again, she spoke.

'Ted fell into the acid lake,' she said. 'And he was down there for a lo—'

'What acid lake?' Yosia interrupted.

'You know the bright blue acid lake in the cave?' she said.

Yosia frowned and shook his head.

'There's a natural cave inside the mine and it's filled with copper sulphate and sulfuric acid,' Molly explained. 'There's an identical lake in the volcano.'

'Is that where you were?' Yosia asked.

'Yes. So we—'

'Who gave you permission to approach the volcano?' Yosia asked.

Molly was surprised by Yosia's question because it had never occurred to her to ask permission to go for a walk. And when walking, one thing leads to another and the next thing you know, you're somewhere strange.

'No one,' she said.

'Did you climb the volcano?' Yosia asked.

Suddenly, Molly remembered the excitement of climbing the side of the volcano.

'Yes!' she said. 'It was awesome and—'

'I'm astonished by your boldness, Molly,' said Yosia.

'What?' said Molly. 'But ... we—'

Michael sat up and looked at Yosia.

'Please don't blame her,' he said. 'We just went for a walk and arrived at the volcano. It looked like something from Mars, so we got curious.'

Yosia's jaw clenched.

'It's extremely dangerous!' he said.

Molly knew Yosia was right. It was dangerous. It was a miracle she and Michael had survived.

'Yosia, there were no warning signs telling us to keep out,' said Michael.

Yosia lay on the grass between them.

'That's because everyone knows it's dangerous,' he said.

'Well, *we* didn't know,' Michael replied.

'Please don't tell our parents,' Molly cried. 'They'll never let us outside again.'

Yosia sighed.

'Are you saying Ted fell into a lake at the bottom of the volcano?' he asked.

'Yes,' said Molly and Michael.

'The poor boy,' Yosia said. 'That would have been a two-hundred-meter drop.'

'No, he didn't fall from the top of the volcano,' said Molly. 'He just slipped on the edge of the lake when we were returning from the jungle.'

Yosia frowned even more than before.

'What jungle?' he asked.

'The jungle inside the volcano,' said Michael.

'Are you saying you were *inside* the volcano?' Yosia asked. 'Down the bottom?'

'Yes,' said Molly and Michael.

Yosia clenched his fists and muttered something that Molly had never heard before. She thought it must be another language, perhaps several. She had no idea what he was saying, but she could see he had the body language of an angry person.

'Are you angry?' she asked.

'I'm *furious!*' Yosia replied.

Molly felt herself edging away from him. Michael did the same. They exchanged glances.

'You could have been killed!' Yosia hissed.

Molly and Michael looked at each other again.

'We know that *now*,' said Molly. 'But we didn't know it at the time.'

Yosia exhaled, loud and slow.

'Please, just promise you will never go there again,' he said.

'I promise,' said Molly.

But Michael remained silent.

Yosia looked at him.

'May I have your promise, too?' he asked.

Michael hesitated.

'Yes,' he said slowly. 'But only if you'll promise me something.'

Yosia frowned.

'What?' he asked.

Michael nodded.

'Promise me you'll let us tell you what we saw down there without getting angry,' he said.

Yosia nodded.

'All right,' he said. 'After dinner.'

Molly was pleased with the plan, but she still felt worried about her lizard friend.

'Is there anything you can do for Ted?' she asked. 'Just as you brought the dead butterflies back to life - can you bring Ted back to his normal state?'

Yosia sighed.

'I'll do my best,' he replied. 'But I have a feeling Ted's been affected by something—'

Yosia frowned again, then scratched his head.

'What?' Michael asked.

'Unnatural,' Yosia replied.

27

MOLLY HAS A THEORY

Molly lay between Michael and Yosia, staring at the night sky. The view of the Milky Way was almost as bright and beautiful as it had been the previous night. She thought about Ted, tucked up in a blanket under the hot water tank in her laundry. She hoped he would wake soon and eat the mashed banana she had left for him. Michael sat up and looked around.

'I think it's safe to talk,' he said.

Molly turned to Yosia.

'Just please don't get angry with us,' she said.

Yosia nodded.

'Okay,' he said. 'Just tell me what happened.'

As they told their story, Molly started to feel better. But she found it strange that Yosia did not know anything about the acid lake in the volcano or the tropical rainforest or the dinosaurs. The only thing he had known about was the flying raptor.

'We call it the Ropen,' he said. 'Everyone living within a

few kilometers of the volcano has seen it at least once. That's why we know it's not safe to go there.'

'So why doesn't someone shoot the thing?' Michael asked.

Yosia sighed, then rubbed his forehead.

'It's too fast and too intelligent,' he replied.

'But Ted managed to outsmart it,' Molly argued.

Yosia nodded.

'Ted was lucky,' he said.

'Has anyone been killed by the Ropen?' Michael asked.

'I'm afraid so,' Yosia replied. 'I'm glad to say, it's been a few years since the last human death.'

'It's *so* weird,' said Michael. 'Everyone knows the dinosaurs died out millions of years ago.'

'Obviously not,' Yosia argued.

Molly was surprised that Michael and Yosia were talking like this.

'Hang on,' she said, looking at Michael. 'We agreed that place is a science experiment, right?'

'Yeah,' said Michael.

'So, the three dinosaurs we saw must be part of the experiment, too,' she said.

Yosia sat up and stared at her.

'Are you suggesting that someone has artificially created the creatures down there?' he asked.

'Yes!' said Molly. 'Didn't you see *Jurassic Park?*'

'What's that?' Yosia asked.

'It's a movie,' Michael replied. 'Actually, there were several. The first one star—'

Yosia put up his hand.

'Please don't waste my time with rubbish from your

televisions,' he said. 'I will discuss this with Gideon and his family tomorrow.'

'Okay,' said Molly.

Yosia leaned forward and stared at her.

'Please promise me again that you will never go back there, Molly,' he said.

'I promise,' said Molly.

Yosia looked at Michael. The boy held up his hands and leaned back.

'There's no way I'm *ever* going back there,' he said. 'Not if you paid me a million bucks!'

28

TWO FLUORESCENT EYES

Molly had a strange sleep. It was one of those *thinking sleeps* in which she was aware she was sleeping while also telling herself to go back to sleep. She was exhausted and desperate for the type of sleep that would revive her body, mind and soul. But tonight was not the night, she knew. So when she heard a scratching sound coming from the laundry, she felt excited that Ted had woken from his slumber. She tip-toed down the hallway, entered the laundry, then gently closed the door behind her.

'Coming, buddy,' she whispered.

But when she opened the cupboard door, Molly was greeted with a scary sight. A pair of fluorescent blue eyes. They were incredibly bright, like the lights the optometrist had shone in her eyes when he had tested her vision. And the color was exactly the same as the lake in the volcano.

Molly slammed the door shut, then leaned against it, wondering what to do. She felt frightened because she knew the beast inside the cupboard was not the same beast that had been her friend. And the more he clawed at the door, the more frightened she became. She opened the external door onto the landing that overlooked the back garden. Then she rested a large stone against the door to keep it open, hoping Ted would scuttle outside as soon as she let him out of the cupboard.

The plan worked.

Molly sighed with relief as she closed the doors and tiptoed back to bed. She pulled her sheet up to her chin, then gazed at her clock. It was 02:41 a.m. The ice packs she had made for her aching hands were not as cold as they had been when she had first gone to bed, but they still provided some relief, so she wrapped her hands around them. And her eyes were sore, so she closed them for just a moment.

She woke again, at 03:17 a.m., shaking. Her first thought was that she was having a fit, but when she sat up and switched on her bedside light, she saw the walls were shaking and the furniture was moving around her room. The little wooden cupboard fell forward and smashed. Her tiny desk slid toward her bed, and two pictures fell from her wall.

Her mother ran into her room.

'It's okay, honey!' she cried, reaching toward Molly.

But the next shudder made her mother fall to the floor.

'Mum!' Molly shrieked.

Then her father ran into her room.

'Darling,' he said, lifting her to her feet.

They both lunged toward Molly, their hands outreached.

'Come on, girls,' her father said. 'We need to get under the kitchen table.'

Molly felt she was part of a strange six-legged creature as she and her parents shuffled down the hallway. The house was shaking so much, it threw them from one side of the hallway to the other. And piles of dirt fell from the ceiling, covering them all and making it difficult to see more than a step ahead.

'It's an earthquake!' Molly shouted. 'I told you, Dad! I told you!'

A few moments later, she was under the table, and her parents were huddled around her. The house shook again and again, each shake more violent than the last. Molly thought about the wooden stilts under the house.

'Please don't break! Please don't break!' she whispered.

There was a loud *bang!* followed by the sound of something cracking. A tree, perhaps. After that, everything was still and quiet. Molly heard nothing but her own breath, and her parents'.

'Stay here, girls,' her father whispered. 'We don't know how long this will last.'

Molly rested her cheek on the cold linoleum floor, huddled between her parents. How long this would last, she could not know, but she was asleep before she could ask any questions.

29

EVERYONE IS OKAY

Molly felt something on her foot. She shook it away. Then she heard a voice speaking her name. She blinked just once. The sun was bright. She heard her name again. When she opened her eyes, she saw Yosia, crouching on the floor in front of her.

'Wake up,' he said.

Molly felt uncomfortable. Her limbs were tangled with her parents'. They, too, were waking up, groaning and coughing.

'Please get up,' said Yosia. 'All of you.'

'Is it over?' Molly's mother asked, gazing at Yosia.

'Yes, it's over,' he replied, offering his hand.

Yosia gently pulled Molly's mother out from under the table. Then he helped Molly.

'I can't believe we all slept through it,' said Molly's father, crawling out.

'I'm sure it was over before you fell asleep,' Yosia replied.

Molly's father squeezed Yosia's shoulder.

'Thanks, mate,' he said softly.

Yosia nodded.

'Let me make you all some breakfast,' he said.

'Thank you, Yosia,' Molly's mother whispered.

The Marsh family shuffled into the lounge room. Molly was quick to snuggle against her mother on the couch while her father turned on the TV. Her parents' favorite reporter, Eddie Abaijah, was talking about the damage that had been done to some houses. Behind him, the camera showed several piles of rubble where grand houses had once stood. The text moving across the screen said the quake had been 6.2 on the Richter scale and had travelled almost one kilometer below the surface.

'Where was it?' Molly asked.

Her father scrolled through his phone before answering.

'The epicenter was literally at the end of our street,' he replied.

'Really?' Molly's mother gasped.

'Isn't that where all the big posh houses are?' Molly asked.

'Yes, muppet,' her father replied.

Molly thought about the people who would have lived in those houses. Not that she had ever met them, or even seen them, but she thought about them.

'Was anyone hurt?' she asked.

'I don't think so, honey,' her mother replied, staring at the TV.

Molly went into the kitchen. Yosia was in front of the stove, stirring a big pot of semolina.

'Yosia, was anyone hurt?' she asked.

'I don't think so,' he replied.

Molly looked at the kitchen table. For the last few hours it had been a shelter, and now it was set perfectly. She could smell coffee brewing, a scent she hated but one that her parents loved.

'Yosia, is your house okay?' she asked.

'Oh, yes,' Yosia replied, laughing. 'My little hut is on the ground so it doesn't have a problem.'

'What about Michael's house?' Molly asked.

'Fine,' Yosia replied, nodding. 'Everyone up this end of the street is fine, Molly.'

'How can that be the case when the houses down the end of the street are in bits?' she asked.

'The epicenter was right at the end of the street,' Yosia replied. 'Behind that vacant block that you people use to access the mine.'

Molly noticed Yosia's use of the words: 'you people'. She guessed he was referring to the Australian and American families who were mining his country. She felt embarrassed.

'I'm sorry,' she said.

Yosia looked at her. His eyebrows were raised and his mouth was open slightly. Molly knew he was surprised by her apology, so she explained.

'I'm sorry about the mining,' she said. 'We shouldn't be doing it.'

Yosia gave her a sad smile, then carried the pot of semolina to the kitchen table.

'Was this earthquake caused by the mine?' Molly asked.

Her father entered the kitchen.

'Actually, muppet, I think it was,' he said.

He sat at the table. Molly's mother sat beside him, clutching his hand.

'Will you join us, Yosia?' Molly asked.

'Yes, I'm on my way,' he replied.

He arrived at the table with a large glass pot filled with black liquid. The scent of the coffee made Molly gag, which made Yosia laugh. The three adults filled their cups and drank without even bothering to add milk or sugar. That's how tired they were. Molly noticed her father's hair standing on end and the dark circles around her mother's eyes.

'Are you okay, Mum?' she asked.

'I'm fine, honey,' she smiled. 'We're all very lucky.'

'That's probably because of the good work Yosia did on the stilts,' said Molly. 'He applied several coats of varnish to the wood to protect it and make it more resilient.'

Her parents smiled at her, then at Yosia, but neither said a word.

30

PLANNING THE NEW DAY

Molly was putting away the breakfast dishes, and Yosia was cleaning the oven.

'Have you seen Ted this morning?' Molly asked.

'No,' Yosia replied. 'He's no longer in the laundry, so I assume you let him out.'

'Yes, just before three o'clock this morning,' Molly replied.

'That's interesting,' said Yosia, his voice echoing around the inside of the oven. 'Ted wanted to escape before the earthquake hit.'

That thought had not occurred to Molly, but now Yosia mentioned it, she knew it was probably true. She had learned that animals can usually sense things like earthquakes and floods before they happen. And now Ted had transformed into a completely unnatural beast, there was no telling what he might be capable of.

'How was he?' Yosia asked.

Molly sighed.

'Well, I got quite a surprise when I saw him,' she replied.

Yosia retreated from the oven and stared at her, waiting for her to explain. But she hesitated, because she knew it would sound strange no matter which way she said it.

'What?' Yosia asked.

He sounded impatient, so Molly knew she had to tell him. She just did not want her parents to hear, so she stepped into the hallway and listened. The shower was running and she could hear her parents' voices coming from the bathroom.

'Okay, the coast is clear!' she whispered. 'It was dark when I opened the door and Ted's eyes were glowing. Actually, they were fluorescent blue.'

'Blue?' Yosia echoed, frowning. 'But Ted's eyes are brown.'

'They *were* brown,' said Molly. 'And now they are blue. Fluorescent blue. As in, glow in the dark. As in the exact same bright turquoise blue as the lake he fell into.'

'You didn't tell me that lake was fluorescent,' Yosia said, frowning more.

'How could I know?' said Molly. 'I've never been there in the dark. I only know its color. And it's the same color as the lake inside the cave in the mine. And now, Ted's eyes are that color.'

Yosia sat back on the floor, twisting his cleaning cloth into tight knots. As Molly looked at him, she remembered he had said he would visit Gideon to discuss what she and Michael had seen inside the volcano. Then she thought of all the other people living in the little sanctuary amidst the agroforest that she and Michael had wandered through the previous day.

'Gideon and his family,' she said.

'Hm?' said Yosia, looking up. 'Oh, they will be fine. Too far from the epicenter to be harmed.'

'That's good,' Molly said. 'But you were going to speak with Gideon about the volcano.'

'Yes,' said Yosia, standing up.

Then he shut the oven door and marched outside. Molly listened to his giant feet pounding down the steps, knowing he had probably gone for the day.

Her mother appeared a moment later, with her long hair wrapped up in a towel, turban style. She was wearing a pale blue satin nightgown with koalas printed all over it.

'You look beautiful, Mum,' said Molly.

'Thanks, honey,' her mother replied. 'You might want to shower, too.'

'Are you telling me I stink?' Molly asked, pretending to be offended.

Her mother raised her eyebrows, then held her nose. Molly knew this was her playful way of telling her she stank.

'Mum, should we be helping to clean up the mess?' Molly asked.

'That's kind of you, Molly,' her mother replied. 'Don't worry, though, honey. The damage is very local, and the rubble is being carried away by professionals. It wouldn't be safe for us to hang around and get in their way.'

But Molly felt restless.

'What are you going to do today, Mum?' she asked.

Her mother unwrapped the towel from her head and shook it over the balcony. Then she dropped her head forward and ruffled her fingers through her long brown hair, as though asking the sun to dry it for her.

'Um,' she said, her head still upside down.

Molly had often wondered what her mother was going to do with her time during their year in PNG. With her father working so much, and there being no jobs for her mother, she had hoped her mother would not get too bored. Her mother stood up straight, then flicked back her hair.

'Actually, I'm doing some research,' she said.

'What kind of research?' Molly asked.

'It's an anthropology piece,' she replied.

Then she smiled and waved at someone. Molly hoped it would be Michael. A moment later, she heard Michael's voice. And his mother's. Next she heard their footsteps ascending the back steps of her house.

'Hey,' said Michael, stepping inside.

'Hey, dude,' said Molly. 'I'm glad you're in one piece.

'Hi, Molly,' said Mrs. Calthorpe. 'You survived the night, I'm pleased to see.'

'Yes, thanks, Mrs. Calthorpe,' Molly replied.

Her mother rushed into the kitchen and switched on the kettle.

'No coffee for me, thanks, Margaret,' said Mrs. Calthorpe. 'Michael and I are heading off to the hospital to see Henry. We're here to ask a favor.'

'Sure!' said Molly's mother.

Mrs. Calthorpe looked awkward.

'I'll have to deal with a stack of tricky phone calls about the mine,' she said. 'So I was wondering if Molly would like to come with us and keep Michael company today.'

Molly's mother glanced at her. Then Molly glanced at Michael. He seemed happy with the idea.

'Sure,' said Molly. 'I just need a quick shower first.'

31

A SCENIC DRIVE IN A POSH CAR

'Wow, it's like a posh hotel in here,' said Molly, fastening her seatbelt.

Even though she was in the back seat of the off-road vehicle, she felt she was seated somewhere reserved for only the most important people. The seats were so big, her feet did not reach the ground. Instead, they stuck straight out in front of her which, she decided, was fine because there was a lot of room between her seat and the driver's seat in the front of her. Above the headrest, she could see the top of Mrs. Calthorpe's head. Her wild mane of curly grey hair protruded in all directions. Molly thought it looked fabulous.

'You have great hair, Mrs. Calthorpe,' she said.

'Oh, thank you, Molly,' she laughed. 'Make yourself comfy back there.'

On the back of Mrs. Calthorpe's seat, Molly noticed a TV screen. A big one. Bigger than the screen on her laptop. She pressed her fingers into the seat she was sitting on. It was firm but springy and it looked as though it was made from a pale grey leather. The velvet trim around the edges was a royal blue color, the same as the carpet, and there were cup holders on both sides of her seat. The air conditioning was cool, but not harsh.

'Mm, this cool air is nice,' she said.

'Do you fancy a massage?' Michael asked.

'Wha—'

Michael reached into the back seat and pressed a button on the console in the center of the back seat. Suddenly, it made the padding move around inside Molly's seat.

'Oh!' she said.

It felt like nothing she had experienced before. Every muscle in Molly's back, butt, and legs was being massaged by her seat. She closed her eyes and felt herself slipping into a deeply peaceful state. Until Mrs. Calthorpe's phone rang. Secured to the dashboard of the vehicle, she only had to press the green button.

'Sylvester,' she said. 'I'm driving. The kids are in the car. You're on speaker phone.'

'Okay, no worries,' he said. 'Call me when you can. It's getting urgent.'

'Will do!' Mrs. Calthorpe replied.

Then Michael hit the red button on his mother's phone.

Molly felt excited by the change of scenery. This was the first time in a few days that she had been anywhere near the highway. She stared at it again, just as astonished as she had been when she had first arrived in PNG. Along the side of the highway were loads of people carrying things in their hands, on their backs, and on their heads.

'Where are they all going?' Molly asked.

'Market stalls,' Michael replied, pointing.

When Molly followed the direction Michael was pointing, she saw a few tiny roadside shops that were no bigger than her bathroom. They were made from a few wooden poles with pieces of cloth for the roof and walls.

'But who goes shopping there?' she asked.

'It's a local market,' Michael replied. 'The people who live here buy and sell stuff.'

Molly noticed several pigs, dogs and chickens running along behind the people.

'Are the animals for sale, too?' she asked, feeling a sad lump in her throat.

'Maybe the chickens,' Michael replied. 'But the pigs and dogs are part of the families.'

Molly liked the idea of the pigs and dogs being part of the family. And the chickens, too. But she did not understand why the whole family had to visit the side of the highway. It did not make sense to her. But, as her mother had often explained: 'Every culture is different, and there are many differences within each culture.' Her mother had spoken these words often enough for Molly to remember them, and she finally felt she was understanding them.

'Oh! Look at that truck thing!' she shouted, pointing.

It was just as big as the trucks she had seen in the belly of the mine. And it had huge claws hanging off it which, Molly knew, would be for picking things off the ground and moving them somewhere else. And it was travelling in the opposite direction so Michael had to swivel around behind himself to see what she was referring to.

'Wow!' he said. 'I wouldn't mind betting that thing is

going down our street to pick up the pieces of those broken houses.'

'Yeah. Did you see the pictures of them on the TV?' Molly asked.

'I did,' Michael replied. 'And then I walked down the street and—'

'I told you not to!' Mrs. Calthorpe snapped.

Molly felt shocked by the woman's attitude. It seemed sudden and violent.

'What did I tell you?' Mrs. Calthorpe shrieked.

Molly felt her heart pounding as Mrs. Calthorpe shouted at Michael. So she was not surprised when he moved away from his mother and stared out of the window.

Mrs. Calthorpe looked at Molly in her rear-view mirror.

'Sorry about that, Molly,' she said. 'It's tough being a mother.'

Molly had a feeling it might be tough to be a mother because her own mother had told her that a few times. But she did not feel sorry for Mrs. Calthorpe, because she had just been very nasty to Michael. Molly wanted to tell Mrs. Calthorpe that she should apologize to Michael, but she held her tongue, because she had recently learned it is not okay to say *everything* that pops into her mind. Sometimes it is best to talk about something else.

'It looks like we're entering a big town,' she said. 'Is that right?'

'Yes,' Mrs. Calthorpe replied.

Molly noticed a mixture of buildings. Some were flat-roofed ones made from concrete and others were pointy-roofed ones made from wood. The wooden ones, she noticed, had interesting paintings on them. Similar to Australian Aboriginal art, they depicted people, animals and the landscape. The colors in the paintings were mostly brown and yellow with white dots. Molly noticed a sign to the airport.

'Is that the airport we arrived at?' she asked.

'Yes,' said Mrs. Calthorpe.

A moment later, Mrs. Calthorpe took the vehicle off the highway. On both sides of the road, Molly saw nothing but banana trees and coconut trees.

'Where are we going?' she asked.

'This is the road to the hospital,' Michael replied.

A moment later, Mrs. Calthorpe pulled into a carpark.

Molly wondered why it was almost empty.

'Have you been here before?' Molly asked.

'Ye—' Michael started.

Mrs. Calthorpe spun around and glared at her.

'Relax, Molly,' she said. 'I'm not abducting you!'

Michael sighed, then dropped his head into his hands. This, Molly knew, meant he was embarrassed. She felt embarrassed, too. Before she knew it, her mouth was open and words were falling out.

'I know that, Mrs. Calthorpe,' she said as politely as she could. 'I'm just a very curious person. I ask questions about everything.'

'She really does,' said Michael, laughing. 'Literally, *every*thing.'

'Fine,' said Mrs. Calthorpe. 'We're here now, so please get out of the car.'

32

A BIG MAN IN PAJAMAS

Molly had seen hospitals on TV, but this was the first time she had ever entered one. It was all white - the floors, the walls, the ceiling, the benches, the chairs - everything. This did not surprise her, but it did make her feel cold and nervous.

'You guys take a seat,' said Mrs. Calthorpe, pointing at a row of chairs in a square room.

There were posters on the wall about healthcare things that Molly did not understand. Next to the words were pictures of people smiling because their health problem had been fixed. Molly thought that was nice, except for the fact that none of those photos included fat white men with broken knees. She wondered if Mr. Calthorpe was okay, and then she wondered if Michael was feeling nervous about seeing him, and then she noticed one of Michael's legs jiggling up and down. She touched Michael's arm gently.

'Relax, dude,' she said. 'Your dad will be fine.'

Michael sighed, then threw his back against the back of

the chair. Molly looked at the desk with the RECEPTION sign on it because Mrs. Calthorpe was there. She was speaking to someone on the other side of the desk. When she was done, she slapped her hand on the desk, then stepped back.

'Hey, you guys!' she called out 'This way!'

Michael stood up, then leapt toward his mother. Which was just as well, because the woman had already started walking down the hallway. Molly followed the Calthorpes, past lots of rooms, each with four beds. All the windows were open so she could see the outside plants trying to grow inside, as though they wanted to make friends with the people in the beds.

At the end of the hallway was an elevator. Mrs. Calthorpe pressed the button beside its steel door. Not once, but five times. This, Molly knew, meant the woman was nervous or impatient or stressed or excited about seeing Mr. Calthorpe. She did not know exactly what the woman was feeling, only that she felt nervous around her.

When they stepped into the tiny elevator, Molly felt there was nothing to look at, except Mrs. Calthorpe. The woman was making a noise, fiddling with her car keys and tapping her foot. But the tapping was not like someone who was enjoying music. It was more like someone who needed to do something with their foot.

'Are you nervous, Mrs. Calthorpe?' Molly asked.

Mrs. Calthorpe spun around and glared at her. The woman's eyes were wild, like someone who was about to fight a room full of people twice their size. And her eyes were a brighter green than Molly had ever seen before. They looked lovely, but unnatural.

'What?' said Mrs. Calthorpe. 'Hm? No. Thanks, Molly. I'm fine.'

The instant they stepped out of the elevator, Mrs. Calthorpe's phone rang.

'Philippa Calthorpe,' she said.

Michael looked at his mother.

'No,' she said. 'No. I can't right now. Yes, I know, but I'm at the hospital. With the kids. Yes. Yes, I will call you back. Please give me a moment.'

Then she hung up and uttered a swear word than made Michael raise his eyebrows.

'Is everything okay, Mum?' he asked.

But Mrs. Calthorpe did not answer. Instead, she pinched Michael's shoulder and steered him down another hallway. Michael managed to shrink away from his mother's grip then rubbed his shoulder where her fingers had been. Molly was starting to feel angry with Mrs. Calthorpe for being so mean to Michael. She opened her mouth to say something but soon shut it, because they had arrived at Mr. Calthorpe's room.

'Dad!' Michael shouted.

'There's my boy!' Mr. Calthorpe said, opening his arms to Michael.

When the two embraced, Molly thought they looked like Tweedledum and Tweedledee. It was a thought that made her laugh and, after dealing with Mrs. Calthorpe, she needed a laugh.

'Henry, darling,' the woman said, leaning toward her husband. 'How are you?'

Mr. Calthorpe shrugged.

'Could be better,' he replied. 'Could be worse.'

'So it all evens out,' he and Michael said together, bumping fists.

As Molly looked at the big man spilling over the edges of the bed, she thought he looked better than she had remembered him. His face had a rosy glow, and it seemed to have fewer lines. Molly wondered if that was because he'd had a few nights away from Mrs. Calthorpe. Then she wondered how he would be able to get up the steps of his house.

'When will you be coming home, Mr. Calthorpe?' she asked.

The big man shook his head.

'I'm afraid it will be a while, Molly,' he replied. 'Because of my size, it won't be possible for me to get up the back steps for a while.'

Molly felt so embarrassed, she did not know what to say.

Mrs. Calthorpe's phone rang again.

'I'm sorry, folks, but I really need to take this,' she said.

No one seemed to mind when Mrs. Calthorpe stepped out of the room.

Michael gripped his father's forearm.

'I hope you're not too bored, Dad,' he said.

'Not a chance, son,' he replied. 'Too much work to do.'

Molly wondered what kind of work Mr. Calthorpe could do from his hospital bed. Perhaps it would involve talking to people on his phone and reading emails, like her father does whenever he is not at the mine.

A nurse entered the room.

'Hello, Mr. Calthorpe,' she said. 'It's time for your shower.'

Mr. Calthorpe tilted his head to the side and smiled.

'Ah, Angel Beatrice,' he said. 'Thank you.'

A moment later, another nurse entered the room, pushing a strange contraption. It was a triangle shaped thing with wheels on the bottom and a huge piece of folded cloth at its center.

Michael frowned.

'What the heck is that?' he asked.

'It's called a hoist,' Beatrice replied. 'It's for moving your dad around.'

Michael's eye filled with tears and his bottom lip quivered.

'It's only until your dad's knee has healed,' she said.

'When will that be?' Michael asked, his voice getting thrill.

Mr. Calthorpe patted Michael on the arm.

'It's fine, son, honestly,' he said.

Molly noticed Beatrice had not answered Michael's question. How long were they expecting to keep Mr. Calthorpe in hospital, she wondered? For a moment, she felt nervous for the man, then realized it might be the best for him to have some more time away from Mrs. Calthorpe and all the problems in the mine.

Molly stood back and watched the nurses slide the hoist over to Mr. Calthorpe's bedside. The device was enormous, as was the piece of cloth hanging from it. But the man was even bigger. She could not watch, so she stared out of the windows. But the two men in beds beside the windows seemed to think she was staring at them, which made her feel even more awkward. And she could hear the cloth being moved and pulled around Mr. Calthorpe. Then she heard him whimper in pain.

'Sorry, Mr. Calthorpe,' said Beatrice. 'We'll keep that knee as stable as we can.'

Molly could not help it. She had to glance at Mr. Calthorpe. She could not see his knee because his long pajamas covered his legs. His face turned red as they secured the buckles around the cloth. Molly did not know if that was because he was in pain or because he was embarrassed about being hoisted up like a giant baby in a nappy. She only knew that she felt embarrassed, so she stepped into the hallway.

Leaning against the wall, Molly stared down to the far end of the hallway and someone mopping the floor. She wondered how long it would take for them to reach where she stood. To entertain herself, she counted the number of rooms between that person and Mr. Calthorpe's room. But that soon got boring, so her mind wandered. And that's when she heard Mrs. Calthorpe. She could not see the woman, but she recognized her voice.

'Yes, I know the chem analysis is concerning,' she said. 'Yes. Yes I know!'

Molly knew this was one of many unpleasant phone calls that Mrs. Calthorpe had to take with her job. She knew she would not be able to understand much of it, but she listened carefully because there was nothing else to do.

'Well, we've discussed that seismic activity before,' Mrs. Calthorpe continued.

Molly knew that 'seismic activity' was about the movements in the earth during the time of an earthquake. Her father had confessed to her that the activity of the mine had caused the earthquake, so it was only logical that Mrs. Calthorpe would be answering questions about it.

'No!' said Mrs. Calthorpe in a sharp voice. 'It's not up to me to record the activity! It's up to government departments and scien—'

Mrs. Calthorpe stopped talking, which probably meant the person on the other end of the phone was yelling at her.

'Fine,' she said. 'Fine. I'll handle it.'

For a moment, there was no more talking. Then Mrs. Calthorpe swore again.

'Off we go!' said Nurse Beatrice, wheeling Mr. Calthorpe out of the room.

When Molly saw the enormous man swinging through the air in that giant nappy fastened to the triangle thing on wheels, she did not know whether to laugh or cry. It reminded her of the awful scene she had witnessed in the mine, when the excavation crane had lifted him onto the haul truck. Michael followed the strange contraption out of the room, his eyes welling with tears.

'Sorry about this,' he said, glancing at Molly. 'I'll be back in a while.'

'Oh, hey, it's cool,' Molly replied.

One of the bedroom doors opened, and Mrs. Calthorpe stepped out. Her eyes were watery from crying, and her thumb was bleeding around the nail bed.

'May I get you a band aid, Mrs. Calthorpe?' Molly asked.

'Hm?' said Mrs. Calthorpe.

She looked down at her hand.

'It's nothing, Molly,' she said. 'But thank you.'

Then she stuck her thumb into her mouth and followed her husband down the hallway.

33

THINGS GET COMPLICATED

Abandoned in Mr. Calthorpe's room, Molly felt awkward. She was aware of the other three men in the room. Two were sleeping, and the other was sitting up, looking around. She got the feeling he might be bored, and in need of someone to talk to, so she disappeared behind the curtain around Mr. Calthorpe's bed.

All she could do was wait for Michael. And while she was waiting, Mrs. Calthorpe's words replayed through her mind. While on the phone, the woman had said something about the chemical analysis being 'a concern'. Molly could not help but wonder what that meant, so she thought about the thing she had learned about chemistry during the last few days.

The first had been the slurry which, her father had explained, was the liquid left over from the water and sulfuric acid they injected into the ore to remove the copper. But that slurry was safely contained, in a secret location in the jungle, and it was regularly checked, her father had told her. He would never lie, so perhaps there was something he did not know about the way the slurry was being kept.

The second thing Molly had learned was about the bright blue lake inside the cave in the mine. Her father and Michael's father had said it contained too much sulfuric acid and copper sulphate for anything to grow. So why would anyone be worried about that, she wondered. Unless they knew the lake had appeared somewhere else.

And then she wondered if that toxic lake had appeared in other places. What if it was contaminating the crops around the volcano, she wondered? Or the drinking water? Anything was possible, she knew, and that was terrifying. She felt an urgent need to share these concerns with Michael. And Yosia. And her parents. And anyone else who would listen.

A *brring!* sound came from Mr. Calthorpe's bed. Molly knew it had to be the man's phone. She also knew it was none of her business, but before she knew what she was doing, she reached under the sheet and grabbed the phone. The screen was still alight from the incoming message.

It read: *Chem analysis failed acceptance test. Meeting tomorrow.*

Then another message appeared: *Slurry leach identified by media.*

Then a third message: *Mining activity blamed for seismic instability.*

Molly was still staring at the phone after the screen had returned to its dark state. No matter which way she thought about these messages, she knew the people running the mine were about to be in big trouble. No wonder Mrs. Calthorpe was in such a dreadful mood, she told herself.

Then she heard Mr. Calthorpe's voice at the entrance to the room.

'Thank you, ladies,' he said. 'I feel like a new man.'

Molly threw the man's phone under his bedsheet and sat up straight. The sight of the big man held suspended in the air by the piece a cloth in the hoist was still unpleasant, but Mr. Calthorpe did not seem to mind.

'Hello again, Miss Molly,' he said with a cheery smile.

'Hello, Mr. Calthorpe,' Molly replied.

'Sorry to leave you alone for so long,' said Michael.

Molly just smiled, shrugged, then sidled out of the room. She leaned against the hallway wall, hoping the visit would soon be over. With nothing else to do, she stared down the hallway. The same person she had seen before was still mopping the floor, slowing making their way up to Mr. Calthorpe's room.

From the edge of her vision, Molly saw a large shape in a crimson robe shuffle toward her. She did not want to know who it was, nor did she want to speak with them. She just wanted to go home. But the person was now so close to her, she had to look. And when she did, she felt her stomach churn. It was Jimbo, the most unpleasant person she had ever met. He stood beside her with his hands in the pockets of his robe. His round face matched the color of his robe. His thick nose was bent and his lips were curled into a sneer.

'What do you want?' said Molly.

Jimbo raised his eyebrows and pursed his lips.

'Is that the right way for a young lady to speak to a gentleman?' he asked.

Molly scoffed.

'You're not a gentleman,' she said. 'In fact, you're the rudest man I've ever met.'

Jimbo laughed so much his belly wobbled up and down. Then suddenly, the smile fell from his face and the light in his eyes went out. His face was completely without expression, like someone who had just died. It was creepy.

Molly shuffled closer to the door of Mr. Calthorpe's room, where she could hear the man speaking with Michael. She wanted to return, but Jimbo placed his hand on the wall, blocking her entry.

'What do you want?' she asked again.

Jimbo lift his chin but kept his eyes on Molly. Looking down his nose at her, his mouth curled into another sneer, one more ugly than the last.

'I want to tell you a secret,' he said.

'What's that?' said Molly.

'The secret is - I know what you're up to,' he said, smirking.

Molly did not know what Jimbo was talking about. She could feel herself frowning. Then Jimbo nodded.

'You've been sticking your pointy little nose where it does not belong,' he said.

Still, Molly did not know what Jimbo was talking about. He could not possibly have known that she had just read the messages on Mr. Calthorpe's phone because she had the curtain closed. She felt her whole face scrunch into a frown.

'I seriously do not know what you are talking about,' she said.

'Really?' said Jimbo.

'Really,' Molly replied. 'Now, if you'll excuse me—'

But Jimbo kept his hand on the wall, blocking Molly's

entrance to Mr. Calthorpe's room. Then he brought his face even closer to Molly's. So close, she could smell cigarettes on his breath. It was a stench that she absolutely hated. Even worse than the smell of coffee. It was so bad, it made her cough. She held her nose.

Jimbo laughed at her. It was a laugh every bit as cruel as the last time she had heard him laugh. The sound was like a crackling fire at first, then descended to a deep and wheezy cough. Molly stepped sideways. Then Jimbo pressed his other hand against the wall, completely trapping her between his arms.

The only way she could escape, she knew, was to kick him in his private place. If she got him, it would hurt him and she would escape. But if she missed, he might get even more nasty. She did not know what to do. He brought his face even closer to hers, making her gut heave with disgust.

'Do you know what happens to nosey little girls?' he asked.

Molly did not respond. Jimbo lifted his hand to Molly's face. She saw the yellow stains on his fingertips and she smelled his stink even more than before. A pool of vomit rose to the back of her throat and she told herself that, if she really vomited, she would aim it all over Jimbo.

'Little girls who stick their noses in other people's business lose their noses. Just. Like. This!' he said, pulling Molly's nose.

'Ow!' she shouted. 'Let me go!'

But Jimbo did not let go. He kept hold of her nose, so she had to breathe through her mouth. Then he leaned in so close to her, his enormous belly pressed against her.

'You're gross!' she gasped. 'Let me go!'

But Jimbo did not let go. Molly could see there was no one else around, except for the skinny young man who had been mopping the hallway floor. He was right behind Jimbo now, but he did not seem to notice the awful situation Molly was in. If he did, he was choosing to ignore it. Molly felt desperate, so she was relieved to hear Mrs. Calthorpe's voice.

'Jimbo!' the woman called out.

Jimbo spun around, smiled and waved at Mrs. Calthorpe. Molly stepped away from him, but she still could not get around him to enter Mr. Calthorpe's room. She was stuck in the hallway, witnessing this strange interaction between the two most frightening adults she knew. If they were to argue, she thought, they would not be very different to Ted and the dinosaur rhinoceros fighting in the jungle.

'Philippa!' said Jimbo, his voice as soft as honey. 'How are you?'

'Get away from Molly!' said Mrs. Calthorpe.

Jimbo put his hands up, like someone with a gun pointed at them.

'Hey, Philippa, there's nothing going on here,' he said. 'We were just talking about Henry. His surgery was a terrific success, I hear.'

Mrs. Calthorpe sighed, then nodded.

'Yes, he's doing well,' she replied. 'But I'm dealing with a few problems at the mine. Can I discuss them with you?'

Jimbo's chest puffed up even more.

'On my way,' he said, stepping toward Mrs. Calthorpe.

But he stepped so suddenly, his bare foot slipped on the wet floor. For a moment, he was doing the splits. He lifted his arms away from his sides, trying to balance himself, but one of his hands hit the wall. This made him fall forward, face first, onto the floor with legs spread wide open. And then he farted. It was a high-pitched squeaky sound.

'Oh, Jimbo!' said Mrs. Calthorpe, scowling.

Then the sound of Jimbo's fart changed pitch to a deeper sound, like a very large dog growling. It seemed to go on for several seconds, then finally ended with a wet, sloshy sound.

'Oh, Jimbo, you're disgusting!' said Mrs. Calthorpe.

Molly made a fast escape by jumping over Jimbo's lumpy body. A moment later, she was standing beside Michael at Mr. Calthorpe's bedside.

'What was all that noise out there?' Michael asked, frowning.

'You really don't want to know,' Molly replied.

'Well, where did you get to?' Michael asked.

'It really is best that I tell you later,' Molly replied.

She felt delighted that Jimbo had disgraced himself in front of Mrs. Calthorpe, but horrified by the way he had pinned her to the wall and spoken to her. Her legs were still wobbling with fear from the encounter. She was also trying to understand what he had meant when he had accused her of being nosey. More than anything, she wanted to return home to the safety of her garden and tell Michael everything.

34

MOLLY TELLS MICHAEL EVERYTHING

The sky was still blue, but with a gold tinge toward the horizon line. Watching it change color as the sun slowly set was one of Molly's favorite things to do. Seeing the light change across the garden and hearing the insects change their songs was another. These things gave her a feeling of deep peace and comfort. And she felt relieved to have told Michael everything - Ted's glowing eyes, his escape from the house just before the earthquake, Mrs. Calthorpe's phone call, Mr. Calthorpe's text messages and Jimbo's bizarre behaviour in the hospital.

Michael sat beside her, more quiet than usual.

'That's a lot to take in,' he finally said.

'I know,' said Molly.

'If I was to piece it all together, I might conclude that the people who own the mine are responsible for the slurry leach, the chemical lake in the volcano, the weird plants and animals down there, Ted's eyes changing color and the earthquake,' said Michael.

'Me too,' said Molly. 'But it's all too strange.'

MOLLY TELLS MICHAEL EVERYTHING

Michael pulled at a thick piece of skin around one of his cuticles, making it bleed.

Molly slapped her hand over his.

'Don't!' she said. 'It's gross!'

Michael's mouth gaped open as he stared at her.

'I didn't even know I was doing it,' he said.

'I know,' said Molly. 'Your mother did the same thing to her thumb today.'

Michael picked a few blades of grass from the ground, tossed them aside, then picked some more. A few moments later, there was a bald patch on the lawn, revealing a little brown circle of soil.

'You've just done it again,' said Molly, pointing at the destruction.

'Argh!' Michael gasped, clenching his fists.

'It's okay, dude,' said Molly. 'That's the kind of thing people do when they're stressed.'

'Yeah,' Michael said. 'It's just really hard to think of my parents as—'

'They might not have known these things until now,' said Molly. 'The people who own the mine are to blame, not our parents!'

Michael scratched his head, which made his thick hair stand straight upright.

'That Jimbo sounds like a real creep,' he said. 'I'd have told him to shove off, if I'd seen him treat you like that.'

'Thanks, Michael,' said Molly. 'And now that I think about it, I wonder why he was in hospital.'

Michael groaned.

'Apparently he's been saying he hurt his back when he lifted my dad the other day,' he said.

'What a load of rubbish!' said Molly. 'He's just trying to get time off work.'

Michael stared at Molly for a moment.

'Are you going to tell your parents what Jimbo did and said to you?' he asked.

'I will,' Molly replied. 'But first, I want to tell Yosia what I know.'

Michael stared down at the garden at Yosia's hut.

'Yep,' he said. 'We have to tell Yosia *everything*.'

'He's in town right now,' said Molly. 'Let's grab some juice while we wait for him to return.'

35

MRS. CALTHORPE THROWS HER PHONE

Molly and Michael sat at the Marsh family's kitchen table, finishing their drinks.

'I love this combo of carrot and orange,' said Molly, using her finger to scoop the remaining froth from the glass.

'I'm going to spell carrot and orange in burps,' said Michael. 'Ready?'

Molly screwed up her nose and shook her head. But the boy started burping, anyway. He got as far as the letter *o* in the word *carrot,* then stopped.

'Huh,' he said. 'I thought I had more in me.'

'That was quite enough,' said Molly. 'Please don't do that again.'

Michael sniggered.

'Michael!' Molly's father shouted from the lounge room.

'Yes, Mr. Marsh?' said Michael, stepping toward the entrance of the lounge room.

'I just got a text from your mum. She wants you to pop home for a while.'

'Okay. Thanks, Mr. Marsh. I'm on my way,' Michael replied.

Molly saw the boy's shoulders slump and his mouth fall into an upside-down smile.

'Do you want me to come with you?' she asked.

Michael shoved his hands into his pockets and stared at the floor.

'Yeah, I think so,' he said. 'Thanks, Molly.'

Molly called out to her parents.

'Just going to Michael's for a minute!'

'Righto,' they replied.

As Molly followed Michael up the back steps of his house, she realized she did not know what to expect. She watched him reach for the backdoor, then pause.

'What?' she said.

Michael brought his finger to his lips, then pressed his ear against the fly screen door. Molly did the same. She was not surprised to hear Mrs. Calthorpe shouting.

'Henry, I'm not lying!' she shouted. 'I didn't know! I swear!'

Molly saw Michael's shoulders slump. The poor boy, she knew, was distressed to hear his mother shouting again. She wanted to give him a hug, but she knew he did not like hugs.

'No, I didn't know about the slurry leach!' Mrs. Calthorpe shouted. 'Jimbo? What about him?'

Molly and Michael stared at each other.

'Well, no, he's not the most charming person on the planet, but he—'

Molly sighed. She knew if the owners of the mine were up to something horrible or illegal, Jimbo would be involved, too.

'The lake?' said Mrs. Calthorpe. 'Do you mean the lake inside the cave?'

Molly pressed her ear against the door.

'Yes, we've *all* suspected the acid levels were high, but—'

Molly turned her back to the door and stared at the sky. It was a deep blue, almost indigo, except for a few thin threads of gold and pink near the horizon. She saw some movement in the trees around Yosia's hut, and she hoped that meant he had returned from his visit with Gideon.

'That's outrageous!' Mrs. Calthorpe shouted. 'How can the lake have duplicated itself somewhere else? That's the most stupid thing I've ever heard!'

Molly felt a light ignite within her because now she knew for sure - the lake in the mine *was* connected to the lake in the volcano.

'Henry, I didn't know about the erratic seismic activity,' Mrs. Calthorpe whined. 'That's for the Geology Department at the university. You can't honestly be sugg—'

Molly did not like Mrs. Calthorpe, but she was feeling sorry for the woman. Everyone seemed to be blaming her for things she could not possibly have done all by herself.

'Yes, I will deal with the media about the slurry leach and the seismic activity,' said Mrs. Calthorpe. 'But we can't take responsibility for any of it without proper evidence.'

Molly looked at Michael and nodded. That was true, she knew. Evidence would be essential if anyone was going to take the problem seriously.

'Good night, Henry!' Mrs. Calthorpe shouted.

Then she screamed a terrible swear word that made Michael's face turn red. A moment later, there was the sound of something inside the house smashing. Molly got the impression Mrs. Calthorpe had thrown her phone at the wall, but she did not want to stick around to find out. She looked at Michael.

'Do you still want to go in?' she asked.

Michael's shoulders slumped again.

'Yeah, I'd better,' he replied. 'Just for a while. I'll see you later.'

36

ADDING THINGS UP

Molly filled a large jug with fruit juice, then put it on a tray alongside three tall glasses. Yosia carried the tray down to the garden, then waited patiently, as Molly smoothed her picnic blanket across the grass.

'Okay, put it here,' she said, patting the ground.

Yosia placed the tray on the ground, then sat beside it.

'Hey guys,' said Michael, approaching.

'Oh, perfect timing,' said Molly, filling the glasses.

She was quick to try the cool, sweet drink.

'Gosh, that's good,' she said, looking at Yosia. 'What's in it?'

Yosia winked at her.

'Just a special combination of fruits,' he replied.

Molly looked at Michael.

'Is everything okay with your mum?' she asked.

The boy raised his eyebrows, then shook his head.

'She's calmed down a bit,' he replied. 'And she's gone to bed early. Maybe that will help.'

'Fingers crossed,' said Molly. 'Before we tell Yosia

everything, I thought it might be helpful to ask him about his trip to the volcano this morning.'

'Yeah,' said Michael, leaning closer. 'I'd love to know what you found, Yosia.'

Molly filled one tall glass and gave it to Yosia. He took a sip, then sighed.

'I'm afraid my news is not good,' he said. 'Although I've seen Ted and his bizarre fluorescent blue eyes, I believe he's changed forever. It's unlikely he'll ever be the friendly beast we all knew.'

Molly had been preparing herself to receive news like this, but it was still difficult to hear.

Michael sighed.

'Did you see Ted in the jungle?' he asked.

Yosia glanced at the ground for a moment.

'I'm afraid not,' he replied. 'Gideon and I had an encounter with Ted around the volcano.'

'Encounter?' Molly echoed. 'What does that mean?'

Yosia took a moment before responding.

'After you and Michael told me what you had seen in the volcano, Gideon and I decided to see for ourselves,' he said. 'We were terrified about meeting the Ropen, even though you had said it was injured and had fallen into the lake.'

'Especially if there's more than one of those things,' said Michael.

'Exactly,' Yosia said. 'We've never known how many there are because anyone who has got close enough to it has been killed on the spot or carried away by the monster.'

'Geez,' said Michael. 'It would be much worse to be

pulled through the air by that thing, I reckon. You'd have too much time to contemplate your death, wouldn't you?'

Yosia shuddered.

'We felt fine while we were in the jungle because we know the Ropen has quite poor eyesight,' he said. 'But on—'

'Ah, that makes sense,' Michael interrupted. 'I don't think it saw Molly and me when we were laying on the ground at the mouth of the volcano, but it sure saw Ted when he was running up the internal wall.'

'Yeah, well, the wall was a pale pink, almost white color,' Molly added. 'And Ted's such a dark grey, so he would have stood out.'

'Nevertheless,' said Yosia. 'Gideon and I were frightened. But we made it to the top of the volcano and we saw the bright turquoise lake. In between the gas clouds.'

'What kind of gas do you think that was?' Molly asked.

'We couldn't tell,' said Yosia, shaking his head. 'We just lay on our bellies at the mouth of the volcano and stared down to the bottom, trying to understand what we were looking at.'

'So what did you think of it all?' Michael asked.

Yosia frowned, then shook his head.

'We've never seen anything so strange,' he replied. 'And to make matters worse, Ted emerged from the lake then climbed up the wall and tried to attack us.'

Molly scrunched into a tight ball.

'Do you get the impression Ted lives in the lake now?' she asked.

'I think so,' said Yosia.

'Geez, that just doesn't make sense,' Michael said. 'We know the chemical composition of that lake does not support life. So when Ted fell in the first time, we assumed he had died on impact. And when he climbed out, he was in bad shape.'

The three friends were silent for a moment.

'Did you see the Ropen?' Michael asked.

Yosia shuddered again.

'No, thank goodness,' he replied. 'The only creature we saw was Ted.'

Molly had an idea.

'Was it definitely Ted?' she asked. 'I mean, those big grey lizards all look the same, don't they?'

Yosia smiled, then shook his head.

'No,' he replied. 'Each one has different markings, as unique as fingerprints.'

Molly remembered her father had said the same thing.

'Please remember I've known Ted for many years,' Yosia continued.

'Which is why it's so sad that he attacked you,' Molly cried.

The three friends were silent again. The only sound Molly heard was Yosia swallowing his fruit juice. She felt glad to be home, safe, in her lovely garden with two friends she trusted. The sun had almost set, and some stars were twinkling directly overhead. She lay back and stared at the sky, taking comfort in its beauty.

'That lake must have some magic powers,' she said. 'For Ted's eyes to be changed by it, and for him to choose to live there, there must be some dark magic at work.'

Michael scoffed.

'I don't know about that,' he said. 'But I wouldn't mind

betting the Ropen is still alive, despite falling in headfirst with a broken beak.'

Yosia leaned back.

'Oh, I think we can be sure the Ropen still lives,' he said.

'But, getting back to the lake,' said Molly. 'What did you and Gideon think of it?'

Yosia shook his head.

'Neither of us has seen water that color,' he replied. 'We're certain it must be contaminated, and we suspect the contamination has come from the mine.'

Molly looked at Michael, aware he was finding it difficult to accept that his parents could be involved in something so awful as the contaminated lake and the slurry leach.

'It's not your parents' fault, Michael,' she said.

Michael's eyes watered.

'It's truly not their fault,' she said again.

Yosia leaned in closer.

'Could you two please tell me what you know?' he asked. 'It's extremely important.'

37

YOSIA HAS HAD ENOUGH

Molly felt better after she and Michael had told Yosia everything they knew - Mrs. Calthorpe's phone calls, Mr. Calthorpe's text messages and Jimbo's bizarre behaviour in the hospital. She felt satisfied she had not omitted a single detail. But by the time she had finished speaking, Yosia looked worried and exhausted.

'It sounds like Mrs. Calthorpe is being blamed for the slurry leach, the contaminated lake and the earthquake,' he said. 'I find that ridiculous.'

'It *is* ridiculous!' said Molly. 'She's only been working there for a week!'

'And the people who own the mine have been here for years,' Yosia added.

'What should we do?' asked Michael.

Yosia sighed, then pressed his lips together into a tight, angry line.

'I think it's time for us to take matters into our hands,' he said.

If you would like to know what Molly and Michael do next, you will need to read the next book in the series. It's called Jungle Magic.

If you would like to receive the author's weekly emails, which include exciting information about science and nature, you can join her mailing list at her website: vkmay.com

www.ingramcontent.com/pod-product-compliance
Lightning Source LLC
Chambersburg PA
CBHW021438080526
44588CB00009B/586